Zoe Williams writes comment pieces, interviews and reviews. She is best known as a *Guardian* columnist, but her work has also appeared in the *Spectator*, *NOW* magazine, the *New Statesman* and the *Evening Standard*. She lives in London with her partner and two children.

WHAT NOT TO EXPECT WHEN YOU'RE EXPECTING

ZOE WILLIAMS

guardianbooks

Published by Guardian Books 2012

2 4 6 8 10 9 7 5 3 1

First published in Great Britain in 2010 with the title
Bring It On, Baby: How to have a dudelike pregnancy by

Guardian Books
Kings Place, 90 York Way
London N1 9GU

www.guardianbooks.co.uk

A CIP catalogue record for this book
is available from the British Library

ISBN 9780852652664

Text design by seagulls.net
Cover design by Two Associates

Printed and bound in Great Britain by CPI Group (UK) Ltd,
Croydon, CR0 4YY

For C, T and H

CONTENTS

CHAPTER 1

But all I did
was have sex...

How to have an unplanned pregnancy

I am absolutely scathing about women who get pregnant "by accident". No, of course not teenagers, or women from highly religious communities who didn't know what they were doing. Some man told them that was the only way to get it really clean... No, I mean women in their mid-thirties (as a wild for-instance) educated (to pick a qualification out of the air) to degree level, of liberal sensibilities, well versed in the fundamentals of conception and, of course, contraception... When those women get pregnant by accident, I always say, "Yeah, by accident, like: 'I decided not to discuss it with my beloved.' Or maybe: 'I discussed it with him, but did not want to throw the discussion open to a wider audience.' Or perhaps: 'I did not want to have a load of conversations about "trying". I didn't want to discuss my fertility until I'd at least tested it. I wanted to stave off for as long as possible the phase where I become public property and I cannot even have a simple brie martini and cigarette chaser without some do-gooder looking at me funny.'"

"That is interesting, Madam," I always think. "Are you taking folic acid with that accident?"

And I still think that, even though it's now happened to me twice.

All that maturity and education and whatnot can be overridden by a simple quirk of being an idiot: it is impossible to hold in your head two mutually exclusive worries at the same time. There is an aphorism for this, which I shall not insult you by Googling. Perhaps it is, "Only a truly sophisticated mind can hold two conflicting worries at the same time"? No, that's about contradictory positions, which I have no trouble with. I can inhabit the mind of a Basque separatist and a Spanish lawman simultaneously; I just cannot worry about being barren and at the same time worry about getting pregnant.

The first time, I was 34. I'd recently done an interview with the controversial obstetrics/gynaecology duo Susan Bewley and Melanie Davies, about how hard it was to get pregnant after 35, but I cannot blame them. There is a feverish media interest in overblowing the dangers of leaving childbearing too late. This has been the story ever since I started working in newspapers, when I was 21. I remember sitting in conference at the Evening Standard, with this hatchet-faced editor going, "What we want is a serious doctor who's prepared to say, 'Do it before you're 30.' That's the headline." I know why papers do this (the generation of anxiety being a bona fide subset of the print industry, and there being sexual politics going on here, also, which are too obvious to spell out) and I know that a lot of the time it's bullshit. But I also know that just because someone's got an agenda doesn't mean they're necessarily wrong, and you don't want to be that one person they're right about, even if you're one in 120,000.

Where was I? Oh yes. I was 34 and I had just bought a house with my boyfriend, C. "We're just about to borrow this much money," he said, helpfully drawing a ring round the figure, while we sat in a greasy spoon and I told him that bacon makes your sperm swim in the wrong direction. "I would definitely tell you if I thought my sperm was swimming in the wrong direction," he said. "Well," I thought, "a) you might not know, and b) it is more likely to be me malfunctioning, your bacon intake notwithstanding."

These were the things I was thinking. I was not worrying about whether or not I might accidentally get pregnant.

Incidentally, on the issue of the house, you may think that makes me above-averagely functional, for a self-centred career bitch? I can temper that impression by saying the relationship had only been going two years, I had no precedent to speak of for a relationship lasting longer than three years, and the house is a bit of a red herring. I will buy a house with anybody. It is the caution of other people that has saved me from large-scale financial ruin.

Anyway, I was worried that I probably wouldn't be able to get pregnant, or C and I would have different timescales that would never coincide, or that I had maybe suckered him into a massive property outlay without first checking that I could produce young, or, conversely, that I hadn't checked properly what he even wanted in this department. (I remember very well his saying that he thought children were overrated, but I thought that was just one of those large remarks people make on dates, like, "Degrees are a waste of time" and, "Alcoholism is just another word for bad PR.") It is impossible to worry about all these things, and also worry about taking your pill every day, or making extra provision if you've been ill and thrown up, or any of that stuff. Seriously, impossible. Go away and try it, and I shall look forward to meeting your lovely baby. This is why mistakes happen at the very point when people seem too old to make mistakes. I have come so full-circle on the matter that when I look at a friend who's 38, who wants kids at some point but not tomorrow, and yet still takes the pill in a timely and responsible manner – still sees herself, in other words, as an unexploded fertility bomb, the way one might at 18 – I am frankly amazed.

But essentially, I only really extend this loving understanding to my own mistakes.

Everybody else who gets accidentally pregnant, I still think, accident my arse.

It was three weeks into our cohabitation that I realised what had happened. C had gone to Cape Town for work. (He's a geologist. My family, who are mainly deaf, thought when I first met him that he was a theologist. In fact I suspect some of them still think that.) It hadn't been going that well, owing to my new burning sense of injustice. It mainly centred around his always being upstairs, apparently, whenever I wanted to say something to him, so that I often had to shout and sometimes literally had to walk up the stairs. Here's what I thought: a) this was the first place I'd lived with stairs. Maybe the problem was having stairs?, b) he was avoiding me, c) he was making some sanctimonious point about having to work, or having cerebral interests, or even just having a hobby and rubbing my nose in it, while I just paced about the kitchen, wondering whether he wanted a beverage.

What did not occur to me was that I was avoiding stairs because I was tired, and I was tired because I was pregnant.

I ran through almost every conceivable inter-couple scenario, and never arrived at that one.

C also noticed the new atmosphere, but for a man who mentions it every time he thinks he might sneeze, he has a strange stoicism in some respects. "Ah," he thought (I am summarising). "Our relationship has moved from its 'fun' phase into its 'nagging and moaning' phase. It is no longer Liberty Hall." And that was that. He passed not one comment. Possibly, if I'd carried on bitching at him and hadn't turned out to be pregnant, he might eventually have wondered out loud about my thyroid.

But so far he was just chalking it up as the price of maturation. So anyway, he's in Cape Town, and I'm stuck indoors. Listen to me – I'm still bitching and moaning at him. He came back two years, eight months and two weeks ago, and I'm not even pregnant any more. While he was admiring Table Mountain, by the way, I was stuck in because we were worried that the dog might kill the cat (they'd moved in together also, as our bestial proxies, and they couldn't even do shagging to iron out their differences).

This whole week, I was livid. The first night, I woke up at five in the morning wondering whether Sainsbury's Local would be open, and if it was, whether it would have any smoked haddock chowder. The second night... No, if I list every outlandish combination and, more to the point, quantity I ate during this week, it will be boring and it will take a really long time. It still didn't occur to me that I might be pregnant. The dog had an open sore on his nose where the cat kept swatting him, and I wept about that. C's uncle died, and I got pretty exercised about that. I went to Birmingham to see my friend who was on a writing course, and he read me a story by someone else, while I was driving, that was so bad I started crying and had to stop the car. Apart from the tremendous hunger, the principal difference was this awful wellspring of sorrow. I'd never even met the uncle, who was radically fat. Though just because I turned out to be pregnant doesn't mean it wasn't sad that he died.

Anyway, still nothing, no hint, and then on the fourth day a guy came round to do something, and said, "That's nice – you've moved in together, you've got the dog and the cat, all you need now is a baby," and *then* it suddenly occurred to me, and then I took a test. And then I spoke to C, and his reaction wasn't as bad as, say, "Oh no, no, no, God no" but it was probably no more than one shit-boyfriend level above that, and then he came home (let the record show that he brought with him a finger puppet of a giraffe), and then eight and a half months later we had T.

For a little while when T was two, I became the Voice of Late Motherhood for certain Radio-3-or-4 discussion programmes. It vexed me because I always thought I'd been asked on in a quasi-academic capacity for some research I had summarised (plagiarised) about population curves, but that never was why. They always started off going, "So, why did you leave it so late?" and I always started off replying, "I was 34 – I wasn't that late. It's not like I had to go and forage for eggs in eastern Europe." But here is the answer: unless you're born broody, and I'm always surprised by how many people are, there is no good time. There's an obvious upside to children eventually. (Otherwise your fifties are very boring. What else are you going to do – go out on the razzle for your whole life?) But there is no upside to children right now. All you can see from the outside is how much you lose.

Amusingly, you have absolutely no conception of how much you will actually lose. You think you won't be able to read as much; you don't realise you won't be able to read a weekend newspaper again for 1,000 years, and that on the very rare occasions you can, you get so overexcited that you can't concentrate and you end up just reading the Boden catalogue, and when, finally, you read one filthy page of current events, you imagine all the news happening to your child and you feel sick. You think you'll have to reshuffle your priorities; you don't realise you won't get another second's peace of mind until you are dead. But still, the downsides tend to be measurable, communicable and manifest, and also parents complain a lot, so there's never any question mark over how intensively they labour. The upsides, by contrast, are immeasurable and incommunicable, and really too schmaltzy to go into in any depth even if you know exactly what you want to say. It looks like a chore; why would anyone do it without a deadline? Asking a regular-issue woman why she left it so late is like asking her why she filed her tax return on January 31: because you don't get fined till February 1, you dimwit.

(Apparently, if you want to persuade women to procreate in good time, you have to remind them to plan not for their first child, but for their full family. I still don't know where I stand on fertility, as a public health message. It is considered dodgy for a government to take any stance on the ideal age to have children. The Department of Health document on this issue, the National Institute for Health and Clinical Excellence (Nice) Clinical Guidelines on Fertility, expressly says: "The recommendations do not cover how fertility problems can be prevented in the first place." Susan Seenan from Infertility Network UK says: "There are no government guidelines for when a woman should start a family. It would not be appropriate, since every woman's circumstances are different, and many women are not ready to start trying for children in their twenties." I can see the sense in this, but it leaves a discursive space in which the only people talking openly about limits to fertility are newspaper editors trying to spread fear among the over-30s for shabby, mercenary reasons.)

Anyway, never mind all that. I think if you come at pregnancy from this point of view, not as the delicious fruit of all your hopes and dreams, but as a long slog you had to do some time – it's just a shame that time arrived so soon... approached like this, it is an unbelievable pain in the arse. And you say to your friends with kids, "This is an unbelievable pain in the arse" and they say, "Well, yes, you get fat and you can't drink – it's the worst two things that can happen to a woman" but they say it flippantly, like, *obviously* you don't like it, but you also love it. And you think, "Well, no, I don't like it. And I don't love it either."

I won't say I didn't have a single good day. Sometimes I was euphoric, once in Starbucks. Mainly, I felt awful. That's the best way I can account for my pregnant personality, which vied with all my other attributes for the title Least Attractive.

CHAPTER 2
Drinking for two

Why abstinence is for suckers

Being pregnant is inherently boring. That is why all the famous stories that start with someone being pregnant have a USP, like a virgin birth or a serial killer. Other people's pregnancies go at the speed of light: one minute you hear about it and think, "Wow, that was fast/slow/about average" or, "She's old/young/about right", and wham, the next you have a photo of a blissed-out person in backless hospital wear, holding a baby that is a bit scary. Your own pregnancy goes at the speed of a PhD.

Throughout my first one, I was filled with a powerful rage. Of course I flushed out a fair amount of this in domestic arguing, but I needed a bigger canvas. Society treats the pregnant in a certain way. Almost all of it is enraging, but there's more mileage in the stuff that's political.

There's nothing political about people who pat your stomach, or talk to you of nothing but your condition, or ask you questions that are too in-depth, or give you a load of old rubbish about how childbirth didn't hurt when they did it because they'd done so much reading around the subject. Move on, raging cow. If you charge, you will only frighten these people – nothing will change.

The edicts about what you can eat, what you can drink, above all what alcoholic beverages you can imbibe: this stuff is political. From a media point of view, the impetus is the same as putting the fear into women about their fertility: it's all just money, and people like to read things that make them anxious. There's also the element that drama is conflict: pregnancy being, as we've established, very boring, you can spice the whole parade up a bit by setting up a conflict between the mother-to-be and her unborn child, creating a narrative in which her behaviour runs counter to its interests.

It's all nonsense. The total abstention from alcohol, avoiding cat faeces (well, sure, don't eat them), the soft cheese: it's all bollocks. There are many professional, credible, medically trained people who could tell you it's all bollocks, but they tend not to appear on any popular media outlet. Whether that's because it does nothing to enhance their standing as physicians, or whether they're never asked, I don't know.

So the conversation, specifically now about pregnant women drinking alcohol, is dominated by pressure groups against foetal alcohol spectrum disorder (FASD). The Department of Health readily cedes to their pressure because there is really nobody mobilising against them, and it seems like an easy wager. They turn out to be right, you've saved all these wonderful babies; they turn out to be wrong, you've caused nothing more than a downturn in the consumption of the white wine spritzer. I will, however, persist in thinking that women shouldn't be treated like three-year-olds, airily instructed in the way of things with no proper, evidence-based explanation, whether they're pregnant or not.

In May 2007 deputy chief medical officer Fiona Adshead put out this advice: "It's simple. Avoid alcohol if pregnant or trying to conceive." Well, sure, it's simple in so far as there are no hard words in it. But that doesn't mean there aren't other complications, like, for instance, why are you saying this? Why now? Have you any new evidence?

I went on the lunchtime news to make the argument that this was soft in the head. Presumably, they'd wanted someone from the government to make the case *for* this advice, and yet, when the story was actually being discussed in the mainstream media, it is amazing how silent the department in charge was. I was a pregnant boozer with no adversary. So I arrived, and even at that point I looked like a shambles, a fat shambles. Things took a radical turn for the worse when my jacket clashed with their bluescreen and they had to find me another one. Only because I was so enormous, there was no lady in the building, *in the building*, whose outerwear I could get away with, and I ended up in the cameraman's tweed sports coat. Seriously. Leather elbow patches. So now I looked like a fat, shambolic farmer who had just wandered into the studio, perhaps looking for a hog that he had lost.

A courteous Alastair Stewart launched with, "So, how much *are* you actually drinking?" By now sweating and pink like a pig (ashamed by my outfit, and also too hot), I didn't exactly say, more like emitted, "Not very much at all, but that's not the point!" and then everybody in the studio looked scared, like if I got any angrier and more discomfited I would go into labour and have my premature, stunted baby right there on the news.

I came out and a young person showed me to the exit – with a surfeit of self-importance, I thought, considering how many signs there were that clearly said "exit". He turned as he walked, and said in this arch, "We're above suburbia, we're meedja" tone of voice, "I hope everything goes OK. It would be embarrassing if it didn't, now, wouldn't it?" He'd put his finger on something. It's one thing being this incredibly noisy, strident, grating voice in the marshmallow world of procreation, where everyone else is drinking hot chocolate and worrying about the minuscule caffeine content. But if I turned out to be wrong, this would look really, really bad.

How did this argument even start? I want to make some bold, unfalsifiable statements – we want to be more like America, where they have preached abstinence for years, or we're becoming more risk-averse, or we're fetishising the state of pregnancy more, yik yak – but I don't even know for certain that articles about FASD proliferate more now than they did 10 years ago. I only know that I have recently taken notice. A typical piece will start like this: you'll get a case study, describing a child with the full range of symptoms, including mental impairment, very low birth weight and subsequent growth restriction, and a distinctive appearance that includes a small and misshapen head, widely spaced eyes, thin lips and a flat philtrum (the space between the nose and the upper lip). Then it will describe the rapid growth in FASD, without pointing out that this correlates exactly with the rise in binge drinking. Nobody is in any doubt that binge drinking is bad for foetal health; the question mark is over whether or not small amounts of alcohol are deleterious. Then it will say something like, "In America, pregnant women are advised not to drink at all", and then a doctor – who, nine times out of 10, will be Raja Mukherjee of the Surrey and Border partnership trust, will be quoted thus: "The uncertain level of individual risk to the developing foetus, coupled with the possibility of misinterpreting a health promotion message, mean that the only safe message in pregnancy is abstinence from alcohol." The piece, if it's in a quality newspaper, will then rather sheepishly deliver the information that the original case study was the child of an alcoholic drinking upwards of a bottle of vodka a day. A red-top will pass over that.

Before this, the advice from the Department of Health was a maximum of one to two units, once or twice a week. A study in 2006 by the British Journal of Obstetrics and Gynaecology concluded that there was no convincing evidence of adverse effects of pre-natal alcohol exposure at low to moderate levels, where moderate was defined as 84g per week, which is 10.5 units (but, the study author Dr Robert Fraser reminded us, not at one sitting, obviously). The Royal College of Obstetricians and Gynaecologists doesn't openly defy the government guidelines, but there is quite a difference between no units, two to four units weekly, and 10.5 units weekly. There is a backbench bill, which recently reached an unopposed second reading, urging that an abstinence message be printed on all alcohol labels, despite the fact that there is no appetite for this among obstetricians and midwives. How this filters down to frontline pre-natal care depends on your doctor; I had a doctor who said, "My advice is no alcohol, but to friends I say a glass of wine can't hurt." I was just about to say, "That seems nice enough", but then I had to remind myself that, being pregnant, this made me furious. "Oh, great, lady," I fumed. "So we qualify for the fun, lenient pregnancy by being your friend? Otherwise we have to have a square, sober pregnancy? How do we get to be your friend? Do we have to go rock-climbing with you, or is it enough just to be middle class and about the same age?" I can't work out where I got the energy for all this outrage, but one does have greatly increased blood flow during gestation. Maybe that helps.

Why is there no safe upper limit for booze? Because that study cannot be conducted – it can be conducted in rats, but even though you would have no trouble finding pregnant women prepared to drink a glass of wine a day in the interests of research, Dr Mukherjee laughingly points out that no ethics committee in the country would accept that evidence. So not only do we not know much alcohol is safe; we will never know. But this does not translate into "It's all dangerous" – how could it?

Physiologically and sociologically, it just doesn't make sense. As Dr Eric Jauniaux, professor of obstetrics and foetal medicine at the Royal Free hospital in London, points out, "Alcohol is mainly metabolised by the liver, and only what's left will be met by the placenta. The amount that could reach the foetus in a glass of beer or a glass of wine is negligible. I would be much more concerned with breastfeeding and drinking."[1] Jauniaux, incidentally, has been studying transfer through the placenta for two decades, is one of the leading national experts on the matter and yet is never quoted in connection with any of these scare stories. And sociologically, of course, Jauniaux reminds us, "How long have people been drinking wine or beer – thousands of years?" Our mothers, grandmothers etc all drank during pregnancy. That may not be a very scientific measure, but the lack of alcohol-related brain damage in earlier generations does militate against blank credulity.

Our trust is further stretched by the interjection of studies that are just plain daft. Jauniaux quotes a study in Northern Ireland, in which they rang a bell at the mother's stomach, and correlated the baby's movement to the amount the mother had drunk during pregnancy. "This was

1. The difference with breastfeeding is that you can actually get milk-testing kits from the company Milkscreen. I baulk at their mimsy literature – "Why guess, when you can be sure?" – and at the fact that the test doesn't tell you how much alcohol is in your breastmilk, just whether or not it's present. For that kind of information you might as well smell your own breath.

at 28 weeks, when we don't even know whether or not the baby can hear. It was frivolous: you can't base your judgment on that sort of study."

Incidentally, the more subtle dagger above the head of the pregnant boozer is the risk of miscarriage, which is what informs the Department of Health guideline that women who are trying to conceive, along with women in their first three months of pregnancy, should abstain altogether. The National Perinatal Epidemiology Unit, headed by Ron Gray, reviewed the available research in 2006 and noted: "In summary, there were eight studies which examined the effect of low to moderate alcohol consumption on spontaneous abortion. Although five of these reported a significant effect, two [of these] had significant limitations, in one paper the only significant result was among heavy smokers, and the remaining two were of only borderline statistical significance."

The gap here between evidence and advice particularly bothers me, because women who miscarry (which is a lot of women), having not realised they were pregnant for the first few weeks, and drunk alcohol as normal (which is also a lot of women), often feel guilty about it. I prefer people to feel guilty when there is a causal link between their behaviour and a negative outcome, not just a load of smoke and mirrors.

The obvious question now is, what's this enthusiasm for giving women advice that is strict to the point of being unscientific, even fictional – or, if we're going to be generous, quoting "facts" that can be no more proved than disproved?

First, consider Dr Mukherjee's perspective, which is not of foetal research but of neuroscience – he's a consultant psychiatrist. He sees children with behavioural problems, poor concentration, hyperactivity disorder, etc. Foetal alcohol spectrum disorder, without its physical manifestations, is a diagnosis of exclusion, ie once you've ruled out autism, ADHD, this raft of medical conditions whose current prevalence is largely unexplained, then you diagnose FASD. The impact of ethanol on pregnant rats leads him to believe that small levels of alcohol can be dangerous, but obstetrics experts such as Robert Fraser or Ron Gray are insufficiently convinced by the rat information to include it in their findings. Mukherjee nevertheless maintains – I'm paraphrasing, but not unfairly, I think – that when you have this web of often indistinguishable conditions, ruinous to the lives of children and of course their parents, if there's even a possibility that alcohol could be causing any of it, then we should at least stop pregnant women drinking altogether, so we can see what's going on.

You can see his frustration, but from the point of view of the pregnant woman, presented with no bona fide evidence for foetal harm at low drinking levels, presented with physiological factors that contradict even the possibility of such harm, confronted furthermore with studies that are "frivolous", the answer is, of course, "Sod that." The part of his conclusion that is openly insulting to women is his citation of "the possibility of misinterpreting a health promotion message" – what exactly is meant by this? It is based, it transpires, on the fact that self-poured drinks are larger than pub measures – in other words, women don't understand what an alcoholic unit is, so rather than waste time clarifying that, better to tell them not to drink at all.

A message of abstinence, from any kind of substance during pregnancy as well as from sex during teenagehood, does not work. Everybody knows it doesn't work, and I would go one further and say that social conservatives never intend it to work – they intend, rather, with their stringency to effect a severance between the state and the individual. Don't come crying to us if things go wrong. We've already warned you to be perfect.

You could dig and dig and dig around this, and all you would ever find, evidence-wise, is that women habitually underestimate the number of units in a glass of booze, and that 9% of pregnant women drink more than the recommended amounts. But *everyone* underestimates the number of units in a glass. According to one study, home-poured measures are a staggering 237% larger than the measures you get in a pub (though I think there is a case to be made that measures in a pub are not large enough).

So none of us, male or female, correctly estimate a unit, and yet this has no impact on general policy. Nine per cent of pregnant women drink more than they should, and the prohibitionists come out in force. With what other section of society does the government throw up its hands and say, "Some of them aren't doing it right. Let's just tell them not to do it"?

One of the problems here is that pregnant women are traditionally thought to be possessed by a spirit of hopeful altruism, a tactical and tactful withdrawal from the rufty-tufty world of fighting and me-me-me, into a more spiritual place where you concentrate on your lovely baby etc etc. Paradoxically, even though society is well stocked with clichés of the "Don't argue with a pregnant woman" variety, it is considered unseemly, even unnatural, for a woman to fight her corner against the corner of her foetus. So basically, you're not supposed to fancy a drink; if you do fancy a drink, you're meant to put your baby first; if you're not convinced by the evidence, because there isn't any, you're meant to be on the "better safe than sorry" spectrum; and if you're so unconvinced that you don't even believe there is this clear choice between safety and sorryness, you're meant to be so ashamed of your aberrance in wanting a drink in the first place that you don't mention it.

Only rarely will someone in the pregnancy industry who is not literally pregnant stick his or her head over the parapet – Professor Jauniaux, obviously, but also Mary Newburn, head of policy at the Natural Childbirth Trust, with whom I agree on practically nothing else. As she puts it, "It's easy to say, 'Don't drink' to be on the safe side. But to be on the safe side of not crashing you shouldn't get in a car. The question is, is the evidence strong enough to say, 'Don't drink at all?' At the moment I haven't seen that evidence. Pregnant women need more evidence and less advice."

This turned out to be a slow news week, so me dressed as a farmer on ITN was just the start. Everybody wanted a fuming pregnant lady. They wanted a greybeard moraliser saying "no", and a heavily pregnant delinquent, preferably still holding the Bacardi Breezer to which she owed her condition, saying, "I'll do what I like!" So obviously, I got a lot of offers. I was dropping calls from the Today programme to take calls from the World Tonight.[2]

2. This is not true. I don't know how to drop calls. But there was a period of about half an hour during which I was number one on the speed dial for the whole of Radio 4.

27

I almost got myself some cards made saying: Journalist and *broadcaster*.

Next I did Sky News, in which I was supposed to debate with Clare Byam-Cook, the breastfeeding guru. Some researcher had messed up, since the most pressing aim is to get the guests fighting, and we were in total agreement. It wasn't my fault. I do what I say on the tin. I guess they must have assumed she'd be pro-abstinence.

The next day I went on Woman's Hour, and this time I did have a majestic oppugner, Susan Fleisher from the National Organisation for Fetal Alcohol Spectrum Disorder. Fleisher is an alarming American, though she lives here, I think, with an adopted daughter who has FASD. She has quite a good adversarial manner – much better than mine. I get overexcited, I can feel my crappy physiological triggers failing to control themselves: sweaty palms, insane heartbeat, all that. If you had me connected to a heart monitor, you would not think I was taking part in a three-minute health-segment on a mid-morning magazine-format radio programme. You'd think I was burgling a house. Fleisher is much more measured, with an easy, patronising calm that I think of as Martha Stewartish, but on no particular basis (perhaps a racist basis? They're both American). She is alarming because her eyes point in two separate directions. It feels childish to mention this, but I really feel you have an incomplete picture without it.

Jenni Murray was away, by the way, and a woman named Jane Little was covering for her. I have nothing against Little, but she was Washington correspondent at the time, and I got the impression she thought herself too grand for the parochial lady chat. I submit, as a kindness to her, that she wasn't actually listening. Fleisher and I peaked when my squinty nemesis said, "If you look at the information…," I rudely cut in, "But what information? There is no new information!" and Little mediated: "Let's not get too bogged down in information…"

Maybe Kafkaesque is overdoing it a bit, but I threw my metaphorical, and probably my actual, hands up at this point. If you're not going to get bogged down in information, what's the point of talking about anything? Why not just get together and bake a cake?

Afterwards, Fleisher and I attempted a civilised debrief. We were being pretty nice with one another, when she said, "Of course, the saddest cases of FASD are the ones that aren't diagnosed. They often end up committing suicide, because they've struggled with this condition all their lives, and nobody's ever understood them." My conciliatory accord came unstuck a bit, here. "How do you know they had FASD, though, if they were never diagnosed?" "Well, they committed suicide! And you can see it from the way they behaved, in their lives. It's very sad."

For. God's. Sake. I had turned myself puce, flooded myself with cortisol, got up at eight in the morning (this was a big deal because I didn't have a baby yet, remember), filled myself from crown to toe with righteous anger, to have a conversation with this woman who was perfectly nice, probably, but didn't understand statistical analysis at all. I mean, I don't have a degree in it, but at the very least I know you can't take as your sample some people who have killed themselves and posthumously diagnose them with *anything*, except being suicidal.

In October 2007, Nice came out with a document saying it could find no evidence of harm at levels below 12g (or 1.5 units) of alcohol per day. This is way more than none. It put this out to consultation, and in March 2008 came back with revised limits of one to two units, once or twice a week, which had been the chief medical officer's advice before Adshead's abstinence message almost a year before. So, here we are again: Nice is up and down like a bride's nightie, and the guidance elsewhere is no alcohol, or if you want to drink some alcohol, some alcohol. I have turned myself blue, again, even trying to get the Department of

Health to admit that any of this is contradictory. Peter Fletcher, one DoH press representative, said the messages weren't contradictory – they were complementary. "Most women," he pointed out, "want to do the best for their baby." I said, "It's still a curious way to go about a public health message. You wouldn't say, 'Never take LSD, but if you do take it, only take it once a month.' " And he replied, "I think we're trying to be as sensible as possible, under the circumstances, given that the evidence isn't there."

So the CMO's final statement is this: "Our advice is simple: avoid alcohol if pregnant or trying to conceive. This advice could also be included on alcohol packaging or labels. Although there is still scientific uncertainty about the precise impact of excess alcohol on unborn babies, we believe the time is right to introduce a strong consistent approach across the whole of the UK."

Then there are some notes, of which these two are my favourite:

1. "Last year the Department of Health commissioned the National Perinatal Epidemiology Unit to undertake a review of existing national and international evidence on the effects of alcohol on the developing embryo, foetus and child. The principal findings were that there is no consistent evidence that low to moderate consumption of alcohol

during pregnancy has any adverse effects, although there is some evidence that binge drinking can affect neurodevelopment of the foetus."

2. While the scientific basis for our advice has not changed, the evidence base is not extensive and we believe it is possible the previous advice could be misinterpreted by some that it is safe to drink "a little" when pregnant, where "a little" can differ from person to person. Most women do actually stop drinking or drink very little in pregnancy, so a slightly stronger message is aimed at those who do not reduce their consumption to appropriate levels."

In other words, there is no evidence. Where evidence was sought, it didn't match what they were after, so they ignored it. Their advice has changed, as far as I can make out, because women didn't previously understand the complexity of numbers like "one" and "two", and concepts such as "once" and "twice."

Moving back to Nice for a second, they have never clarified why they lowered their advice from 10.5 units a week to one to two units, once or twice a week. I have asked them why they made this change, repeatedly, and they are keeping a dignified silence. Just ignoring me, in other words. What do they think I'm going to do? Get bored? Die? Idiots. Anyway, pending a Freedom of Information request, let's wonder at something else. When, for their secret reasons, they adjusted these guidelines downwards, chief medical officer Liam Donaldson released a statement saying, "I welcome this updated Nice guidance as it further strengthens the advice... that pregnant women or women trying to conceive should avoid drinking alcohol." Well, no, it doesn't. I don't understand this. In what other area of science are the experts regularly trying to insist that "none" and "some" mean the same thing?

Because of the contradictions, the lack of foundation, the irritating tone, possibly the fact that nobody listens to government guidelines, ever, about anything, most of the pregnant people I know made up their own informal structures of drinking, of which my favourite were:

1. Drink like a French pregnant woman. It is actually not true that French women drink throughout their pregnancies. Their stated government line is abstinence. But for some reason it seems atmospherically true that a French woman would have a glass of something if she fancied, but never end up in the gutter. I heard the phrase "I'm having a French pregnancy" quite a lot.

2. Drink like it's your second. Everybody is less neurotic about all the dietary habits for their second and subsequent pregnancies, even though this is irrational, since your only evidence is that everything was fine last time. Not even Nice would base anything on a sample of one. Though I wouldn't put it past Liam Donaldson.

3. Stress is actually worse for your foetus than a glass of wine[3]. I also heard this used as a good reason to smoke a joint, though. And that is definitely frowned upon.

I'm not just a boozer who wanted to drink more booze. If you would like me to be honest about my attitude to alcohol, anything under a bottle of wine doesn't touch the sides, so the difference between no units a week, two, four and 10.5 is no difference at all, unless I were allowed to drink all 10 at once, but even reputable sources counsel forcibly against that. No, speaking personally, I am as impartial in this as a teetotaller. But this is not just alcohol: exactly the same fudged, improperly evaluated scraps of scaremongering are thrown out about coffee, cheese, meat, bagged salad, seafood… Fundamentally, I think the aim is

3. www.guardian.co.uk/science/2007/may/31/childrensservices.
medicineandhealth

to keep us in a fog of guilt and confusion, biddable, supine, feminine. It's annoying. We're already pregnant – how much more feminine can we get?

About three years later, I was lying in bed and it suddenly struck me: they tell you not to drink and drive. When in fact you can drink and drive – just not very much. So maybe I was wrong. Maybe this isn't a conspiracy against women at all. Maybe the forces for paternalism aren't winning, maybe we're not all becoming more individuated and risk-averse and factionalised. Maybe this is just the way things are done. Huh. All that time I could have spent thinking about something totally different.

CHAPTER 3

Every argument my boyfriend and I ever had

From "Who got us into this?"
to "Why can't the baby juggle?"

I was going to group these by theme. Then I thought I'd break them up by who won, with a cross-reference to who turned out to be right in the long run. Structurally monotonous, I'm afraid. I always won, and I always turned out to be right. In the end, I went with chronology, from the moment I realised I was pregnant with T to the present day. It is an imperfect index of gravity, but we're still together, aren't we? (Well, who knows? We are as I write.)

1. Whether or not I had got pregnant on purpose, unilaterally.

2. Whether or not I had got pregnant on purpose, unilaterally, because I wanted to be exactly as pregnant as my

sister. (For God's sake! Half the time he thinks I am an incompetent PA, and the other half the time he thinks I am God.)

3. Whether I was over-eating hyperbolically, for effect.

4. Why I didn't realise that there was something a bit disgusting about watching me eat tinned octopus.

5. Why he didn't realise that, in this dawn of a new era, taking the opportunity to point out that I physically repelled him was just really annoying.

6. Whether or not I was better company, worse company or the same company now I wasn't drinking.

7. Why he kept filling the house with the delicious smell of toast, like some kind of child.

8. Why he was, overall, like this giant great feckless child, and how on earth he was going to be any help to me, if this was what he was going to be like.

9. Who was best adapted to life's arduous parts: a science graduate or an arts graduate. He said that, because his

degree involved lying in a cold puddle for eight hours at a time, whether you wanted to or not, he had more back-bone. I said that because my degree had involved engaging imaginatively with people both real and fictional, I empathised better and was therefore less likely to put myself first. This is a weak argument. Divert, divert!

10. What kind of meaningful scientific enquiry involves lying in a puddle? How can that possibly have swelled the sum of human knowledge?

11. Whether or not he should have discussed it with me before he promised his mother that we wouldn't have children until we were married.

In New York in February, on a mini-break that we'd booked before all this started:

12. Whether or not I probably felt the cold more, being pregnant, or whether my increased blood supply was keeping me warm and I should stop complaining. New York sucks when you're pregnant because you can't drink and you can't shop, and what else are you going to do? And it was *minus eight* degrees. It was so cold you could see your nipples through your coat. I was convinced I was about 13 weeks pregnant, and that I could probably have a baby by summer if I just set my mind to it. This was based on the fact that I'd put on so much weight already. In fact, I was four weeks pregnant; I barely even warranted the title. I was deputy pregnant, pregnant in brackets. It's amazing how much weight you can gain on tinned octopus, if you eat enough of it.

One particularly bad day (of the three and a half) I was alone for an hour. The real reason was that I wanted a meal between lunch and dinner, but I was embarrassed so I confected a reason to storm off. Finding myself in a Barnes & Noble, I bought a book called And Baby Makes Three, by two clinical psychologists, married to one another, John and Julie Gottman. Its subtitle was The Six Step Plan for Preserving Marital Intimacy and Rekindling Romance after Baby Arrives. Unfortunately, I cannot remember any of the six steps; it's possible that I did not even reach any steps. All I got to were the depressing statistics: the proportion of couples who talk about divorce in the year after having a baby; the number who stop having sex; the percentage who talk about getting a divorce *while* they're having sex – which sex, incidentally, is the first sex they've had for a year and a half. The number of men who have an affair; the number of women who report loss of self-esteem; the number of babies forced into the role of peacemaker before they can even talk, who then go on to put their own emotional needs second throughout their lives, only they don't know why because it all happened before they could talk, so they can't remember any of it.

13. This book spawned a lot of arguments, about almost everything. C did not know about the book, however. Indeed, he still doesn't. For some weird reason, I took the dust jacket off.

Oh no, I've remembered why I took the dust jacket off. It's because I went into Whole Foods straight afterwards, and bought a falafel wrap, and spilt hummus on the book. Since I was pretending not to have had another meal, I couldn't very well go back to the hotel with a book that smelt of chickpeas and garlic.

I was incredibly secretive in my first trimester, about everything. I read something about why teenagers are the way they are: their rate of growth exhausts them so profoundly that their brain function diminishes. The evolved segments that they don't really need – frontal lobe functions like empathy, kindness, altruism – shut down, leaving only their reptilian brain in action, which is dominated by paranoia and suspicion. That was pretty much the size of it, because I was paranoid and suspicious and also incredibly tired, like a teenager except not attractive.

One thing I haven't mentioned is that we went to New York with some friends of ours, and this couple does still talk to us. But they like C better than me.

14. So C and I have an argument, as well, about why they like him better than me, and whether he couldn't have refrained from using my temporary insanity as an in to ingratiate himself with the world, and gull everybody into thinking he's the nice one.

Back in London:

15. Whether or not, in the first outing we had since we agreed that we needed more outings that didn't rely on us both being drunk, that first occasion *had* to be Brahms's German Requiem. Is this the kind of show we're running now? Has it really turned out that we have no shared interests apart from booze, so we're going to try and drum some fun out of this piece of incredibly long and boring music, which neither of us even owns on CD or has any attachment to? And so soon? My sister and her boyfriend took to going to country houses in her first pregnancy. So I suppose it could have been worse.

16. Talking of which, who was fatter, me or my sister. (We were at cross-purposes: I meant who was fatter relative to her previous size; he thought I meant who was fatter absolutely. Though I should point out that his answer was still wrong. He should have said, "Neither of you are at all fat, but she looks three and a half weeks more pregnant." I will be waiting a long time before he turns into a boyfriend of that order of perspicacity.)

17. Oh my god, and as if we hadn't learned our lesson going to the Barbican, then we went to the theatre. To see The Entertainer, and we argued in the cab home about whether or not my dad had been a fake and a pisshead, in the manner of Archie Rice. But C never met my dad, who died before we got together, and I think he contended partway through that he hadn't said that or anything like it, and could I not just chill the fuck out for the last 20 minutes of this terrible evening?

18. C was putting off telling his parents, because of the aforementioned promise, but we were going out to dinner with his brother and sister-in-law, and I wanted to tell them, because otherwise, not drinking, I'd look like a killjoy. And here I will concede that I took the drinking/not-drinking thing way too seriously. I thought people would a) notice and b) care enormously if I did not end every social occasion totally toasted. It's not true: all you have to do is order

a drink, and then sit there with it. You can drink it or not drink it. Nobody notices. Get over yerself, lady, I finally tell myself months – no, years – later.

In Jamaica:

So far as I remember this was conflict-free. But it might have just been too hot to argue. C did start smoking again on this holiday, swimming somewhat against the accepted tide when you're expecting a baby, which is to stop smoking. He must have been responding to some stress or other, but could it, I wonder, have been caused by me?

London again:

At 21 weeks, when we got back, we had the anomaly scan and no arguments at all, but that does remind me of an argument I'd forgotten, at the first scan, which was meant to be the nuchal fold test but turned out to be too early.

19. I was 10 weeks; nuchal fold has to be between 11 and 13. I had a tantrum on the way out, because by my calculations of pregnancy (based on scientific markers like when I first got into a bad mood, when I first noticed that my bad mood was hard to shake, when I first conceived a longing for haddock), I should be 13 weeks. Ergo, there must be something wrong with the foetus, since it had sprung into life, stopped growing for three weeks, then started again.

I can't remember much about his response at all, but as I think about it I am conjuring up an image of him sitting there with his head in his hands. It's more of an atmosphere than a memory. There was a lot of that during the first pregnancy – the irrational rages, the health concerns cooked up to create some static around the tremendous pettiness of my actual concerns.

For instance, that tantrum was not about there being anything wrong with the foetus – rather, I was upset that the dating scan showed me three weeks less pregnant than even my most pessimistic estimates, so I was going to spend three more weeks than anticipated still pregnant. Not only had I had no regular emotional response to the sight of a foetus, with a beating heart; I didn't even feel dead inside. I wasn't even depressed. I felt vexed, like I'd just lost my cash card. I had to pretend I thought there was something wrong just to mask the sterility of my interior landscape. It reminded me of being a teenager, the way you back yourself into these absurd positions because otherwise you have to start explaining how shit you are.

The thing is, society en masse does not understand the first pregnancy – it only understands the second one. This is as it should be. Society can't pretend to have no idea what's around the corner, with a baby coming. We've known, collectively, what having a baby is like since the beginning of time. So all the clichés, all the call-and-response stuff ("I bet you're excited!" "I'm *really* excited!" "Do you want a boy or a girl?" "Yes! I want a boy or a girl!") is from the perspective of knowing how wondrous and awe-inspiring it is when it comes, and how it's your blossom and the apple of your eye, and you'd do anything for it. But in your first pregnancy, you're the other side of that gorge. You can't even see the edges; all you can see is the gorge.

Let me amend that, from "you" to "me". I did not feel excited. I was never a particularly broody person. I thought the point of children revealed itself when they were about five and started to make sense. I wasn't worried about the baby and whether everything would be OK; I was worried about my own identity, and my place in the world, and whether I would get along with parenting at all, and all the freedoms I would lose. And my fat arse. When people – medical people – gave me to understand in a word or look that we were all in this together, that we all wanted what was best for the baby, I felt actively hostile. Not only did I feel nauseated by this flowery patchwork of self-effacement and altruism; of course I felt accused by it, because I just didn't feel it. I didn't want what was best for the baby. I had no conception at all of "baby". I just wanted whatever was best for me, and didn't kill anyone else. There is a midwife I would happily have killed as part of my labour, but we will deal with her more fully in the next chapter.

They're a lot easier to conceive, these babies, than they are to conceive of.

Anyway, I think the whole nine months was defined by this awful isolation, which is not unlike the isolation of adolescence. People, adults, might say you'll grow out of this or that, or you'll feel differently after the passage of some or other amount of time, and they'll be right, but it's immaterial. It makes no difference at all to the way you feel. It just makes you feel more aberrant, and more widely rejected. I remember, at some point during the five minutes that we were on speaking terms, telling my mother I felt lonely, and her laughingly pointing out that that's what happens when you only socialise with alcoholics, and then you get pregnant. There is merit in this opinion, but I think the loneliness that comes from feeling that you're outside culture is colder. It gets into your bones, like a Swedish winter.

That was just preamble to the acknowledgement that there were definitely a few arguments we had that, thinking about now, I can't fathom the cause of.

20. I screamed at C viciously once, over some cat poo that he should have cleared up, instead of leaving for me, considering my condition. It would have been absurd anyway, considering my strongly held and often-uttered views on the dangers of cat poo (negligible, overdramatised and easily countered by the simple precaution of not eating it). But worse, this poo was hypothetical. The cat had not shat in the house. The cat never shits in the house, unless you jam the cat flap.

21. Then we had a horrific fight – well, "fight" isn't quite there, since it was mainly me talking ("talking"), but "horrific" is on the money – about his finishing the crossword before I'd had a chance to have a look at it. I was totally savage, like a primate who really likes a cryptic crossword in theory but has no idea whether to solve it, stab it or eat it.

22. We had an argument about why I was spending so much money at the hygienist, but that was just a misunderstanding on his part. My gums were so shot, one of my teeth was actually mobile. It's fine now. I've still got it (the tooth, I mean, not an unknowable quality of sexual allure).

In the third trimester:

My mother has long-term pulmonary damage (You want to know what caused it? Do you? *Smoking*), which she doesn't often complain about, but when – for reasons related not to my thoughtlessness but to the laws of the physical universe – we have to go up some stairs, by the time she reaches the top she is always absolutely scowling at me. It really pisses me off. I neither forced nor encouraged her behaviour; I wasn't even alive for the first 20 years of her smoking career. But she distils pretty well for me the correlation between rage and lung capacity. It's not like the rage of hormones – towering, sudden, then immediately vanished like a March hare. And it's not like the fury of low blood sugar, which is more lumbering and swampy. It's just a scowling, pissy, out-of-my-way temper, brought about by attempting to power more mass on less oxygen.

It was in this humour (more baby, less lung space – you got that, right?) that we argued about:

23. How far Gloucestershire is from Sheffield (we've got satnav!).

24. Whether Kate Moss is prettier than me (to put that in context, we were in a pub called the Swan in Southrop, where Kate Moss lives, and I said something about possibly seeing Kate Moss, and C let out some "pff" that I chose to interpret as, "Someone that pretty would never come in here..." I don't want you to go away thinking that I just threw down that gauntlet: "Who is prettier, me or Kate Moss?" I'm only pregnant. I'm not insane.

25. Whether he should have stayed sober the night before the parenting class, ie treated it like an important meeting, or whether it was fine to have a stinking hangover because it was just a load of total idiocy, where a woman says, "Write down all the things that you think make a good parent" and the hippy next to you writes, "Giving a child space to grow and explore his or her own personality, and not constantly telling her how to think."

26. Whether he had to go to the labour workshop at all.

27. Whether he was allowed to go to see the Police in Cardiff the week after my due date, when he'd have seen them at Twickenham two weeks before anyway. Whether Sting would even appreciate loyalty like this, or whether, contrariwise, he'd think it was weird. Sting would probably, if he knew, write a song about how fucking weird that was, leaving your girlfriend and new baby to see the Police, when you'd *only just seen them*.

28. Whether it was in the baby's best interests to try to force it out with raspberry leaf tea at 39 weeks, and whether or not he could give me his stupid views when *he*'d spent the past eight and a half months growing it.

29. The labour itself was remarkably conflict-free, and we didn't have an argument at all until immediately afterwards, when he was meant to be cutting the umbilical cord but was instead texting. He looked like a sodding teenager, playing Tetris while I quite literally brought life into the world. He said he was texting our nearest and dearest to tell them we were all alive. I spoke to a friend a few months later, who had this argument with her husband after the birth of their third daughter, even though they'd already had it after the birth of their second. (When their first was born, mobiles didn't exist. That's how long this argument has been happening, between a man and a woman: since the dawn of mobile phones.)

This isn't an argument, just an aside: the hospital, St Thomas', was right opposite the Houses of Parliament, onto which you get a view if you "opt" not to have any pain relief. (I have another friend who had a baby there just before Christmas, and didn't get just the seat of democracy, but also fireworks. The dads always go on and on about the phenomenal views, and the mothers always sit there making a face like, "If this chimp tells anyone about the view one more time when I might as well have been staring into the mouth of hell, I am going to kick him to death.") Anyway, so the text C sent when it looked like he was playing Tetris read: "Healthy baby boy, born 11.24 by the hands of Big Ben". And C's mum thought we had a big midwife called Ben.

Home again with T:

30. We probably did have an argument in the first week, but I can't remember it; all I can remember is a state of bizarre, intense bliss, and not getting time to clean my teeth, but I can't remember why not. In the second week, C remarked that it was weird how, on the birthing videos, they can recognise their dad's voices and mimic faces, whereas ours didn't seem to be able to do anything at all, totally blank-eyed, totally vulnerable, like a hedgehog we'd found at the bottom of the garden. And I thought he was calling T retarded and took myself onto the roof terrace to breathe deeply, so that I didn't try to kill him. And I counted to, like, 143, before I realised that the counting wasn't working, and just came back in.

31. I embarked on a massive row when C went to the Norwegian town of Stavanger, only a week after he got up at 4.30 in the morning to go to Aberdeen. I was so half-blind with outrage that it was all I could do to get out the words "Aberdeen", "Norway" and "4.30 in the morning" before I crashed into a wall like a concussed bull, so that for the first five minutes of the conversation he actually thought I was sympathising with him for having to get up early.

Under interrogation, I revealed: no, I did not want him to stay at home, nor catch a different flight, nor get up later or get home earlier, and no, this was not about his carbon footprint. No, I didn't want to go to Aberdeen myself, nor Norway. I didn't want to get up at 4.30 myself, and I didn't resent his complaining about being tired when I was up three times of every single night, although I think if you were to get something really painful underneath my fingernails, I might admit that I resented this a little bit. You'd think there's no limit on how many people in a household are allowed to be tired, but apparently there is. No, I didn't want him to give up work and hang around me and T the whole time. No, I didn't want to go *anywhere* myself: even if it were Maui and not Aberdeen, I still wouldn't have wanted to do it. I just looked at his freedom of movement and I held it against him. There's no other way of putting it. I didn't want that freedom of movement for myself, because that would have meant not having T, who was the best thing that had ever happened to me. But it seems that even not wanting it myself, I urgently wanted C not to have it, either.

This is what the word churlish was invented for. I'd lost a penny and found a pound, but the very small part of me that missed the penny required C not to have any money at all. Maybe he could have a button or something.

And yet at the same time, the reason it gets to you is that it's so unfair and it's such a cliché. For the first six months, the mother looks after the baby. The father can show willing or be an arse about it, but in a way, it's even worse when he helps because it makes you realise that it's not even his fault when the buck stops with you. It's just an eternal verity: there is a buck, and you are where it will stop. You do start to wonder, was gender equality just a bit of fun to occupy you in your twenties, like university? Was it all a sick joke?

I think this is why your proto-feminist, your mother's-generation women's libber, is always so hard-boiled about babies, so determinedly unsentimental, so liable to say things like, "Childcare is no kind of work for an intelligent woman." I thought they were just being daft. Who can seriously not like babies? How can it possibly undermine your intelligence to admit how much you love them? But they just realised earlier how incredibly hard it is not to slip into a 1950s housewife role. It's one thing looking after the children;

admit that you enjoy it, and you're toast. All your dreams of the workplace, your O- and A-levels? Toast.

32. After that, C developed a new habit of saying, whenever he went anywhere, including to work and to the loo, "Do you mind if I exercise my freedom of movement and…?" So we had a number of arguments about whether or not that was funny.

33. We had argument after argument about room temperature in our bedroom. We also argued quite a bit about when the baby would be moved into his own room, but before that…

You're meant to have it really low otherwise babies catch cot death, and yet you can never get it low enough without freezing your ever-exposed tits off, and C said, "What this room needs is a throughput of air", and I thought he said "a Rupert the Bear", and normally I would think, "Well, I have just misheard my beloved", but on this occasion, I thought, "This idiot! How would Rupert the Bear help? How would we even get hold of Rupert the Bear?"

34. It seems strange now we've got our second, and never argue about this at all, but we had a number of skirmishes about T's development, and whether it was on track, whether I was trying to hothouse him (such rubbish! Why would I do that, after all those in-uterine months trying to retard him with booze?), whether or not he was too young for opera. Between about three weeks and maybe a whole year, every time T smiled, C would go, "It's just wind." I ended up thinking, this poor kid, when he graduates, C will be standing at the back going, "That's not a degree, that's just wind…"

Once he had a little growth spurt. I looked up "growth spurt" on Mumsnet, and somebody said it was often followed by a new skill, like rolling. That's what they need the extra food for. Sure enough, and when I say as if by magic, that's really how it felt, at the end of it he was rolling. "Look, look!" I said. "It's the new skill!" "I was hoping it would be juggling," said C. "What are you saying? You mean man! You think we have a slow baby! No babies can juggle!"

35. C had this really annoying habit where he didn't want to be part of any administrative conversation until the task had already been 75% completed. So I'd say, "We can do a childminder, a nanny-share or a nursery," and he would say, "Which is the closest?" And I'd say, "I don't know, you lummox, I haven't started looking for any of them until we decide which one we want." And he would say, "It would be good to know which one is closer", and at that point I would either become so exasperated that I stormed out, or my mind would wander and I'd forget what we were talking about.

Generally, I'd say the resentment you (I mean me – take it as read, why don't you, that I always mean me) feel towards your beloved is not baseless – it just occupies that uncomfortable spot where he is its focus and yet it is not his fault. As relatively free (I'm still on about freedom of movement) as I am now, I'm still bound by my own feelings. I cannot do my own thing, like, I don't know, stay for a drink and have it become five drinks, or spend a week cycling round Austria for work, or drop everything for a really important meeting in Darlington (of course I'm being hypothetical. What kind of meeting would they have in Darlington? Plus I am never invited to any meetings). We can plan a weekend away from T and H, our second – indeed we have, and it's been fine – but any longer would be counterproductive because these mini-breaks are meant to be fun, and I wouldn't be having any fun.

It's the spontaneity that's gone – that's what I miss. Not the events of yore particularly, but the life that accommodated them. And I don't feel that C's spontaneity has taken the same thrashing. But that's irrelevant – if he were tied to the home by a million threads of guilt and longing and groundless fear, it wouldn't make me any freer. What I need is not for him to be better, but for there to be two of me. He can't help with that at all. But he could at least look as if he were trying.

CHAPTER 4
The fog of birth

Why labour is no big deal
(especially when you're unconscious)

Here is something I've noticed about labour: before it, even though the world is awash with people telling you what it's like, you get the constant impression that you're missing something vital. When you've done it, you look back and realise that everything that happened, somebody, at some point, had told you would happen, but nobody put the information in the right order, and they failed to really stress the important bits. They will tell you curiosities – like, perhaps you will get (literally) cold feet, and this can be countered by (literally) wearing socks – with more energy than they tell you about the main bits, where an actual baby comes out.

Imagine if somebody rewrote Paradise Lost, with 3,000 lines about the serpent's interesting colouring, and then half a page of descent into hell. It would be vexing, wouldn't it?

Yet the orthodoxy is that you do pregnant women a kindness by sparing them horror stories: any accurate account of childbirth is, by definition, a horror story, apart from my friend who said it was like having an orgasm, ergo you spare a birth-novice the account, or if they really press you, you scramble it in such a way that all they hear is, "Yik yak yik yak, ooh, that wasn't very nice, never mind, annoying husband/boyfriend, nearly there, *lovely baby!*"

So all the way through pregnancy number one, I am thinking, I can't wait for this to be over so I can be normal again, and then two weeks away I realise that two weeks is nothing like far enough away from an event that leaves a significant proportion of women (one I read about in Easy Living, and one friend of my sister's) suffering post-traumatic stress. I am clinging onto the orgasm remark, and another double-sourced eyewitness statement, which is that labour is not hell; it is not pain; it is merely, as the name describes, very hard work. Think of a marathon, or an incredibly large coffee stain before the advent of mechanised laundering. So I've got those in my think-positive column.

In the other column, I have: one friend who said that women can sometimes go feral, because they connect a little bit too deeply with their inner beast. If this occurs, you mustn't look them in the eye, because they'll interpret it as a threat and kill you with their (unvarnished) nails/claws.

You have to do something submissive, like show them your neck. Another told me a story about her labour while she happened to be sitting next to her birthing partner (she'd planned to have it at home, then had to get an ambulance 19 hours in when the foetal heartbeat stuttered).

"So I had to get into the ambulance, in the middle of crippling contractions…"

"Naked, into the ambulance…"

"I was not naked!"

"What do you think you were wearing?"

"Something! I was wearing something!"

"I can tell you, you were not"

(It's not that she lacked the modesty for clothes – that could happen to anyone. It's that she didn't *know*, she has no memory of whether she was naked or not. That is not life, that's a dream, a trauma, a half-buried account of war. And plus, how much more feral do you want?).

I have plenty more in this negative-thinking area, but I am straying into the territory of needless terror-mongering. Don't worry about it, basically. You will probably be fine. But this is what my first time was like.

To go into labour, first you need to bring it on. There are probably 1,000 methods with a cheerleader, somewhere, telling you they work, but if anything actually did work, we would no longer talk about it. Someone would have written it down and that's what we'd all do. Incidentally, although I have no statistical evidence of this, I have met more people who claim curry works (two), than who have been successfully induced using oxytocin and not ended up having a caesarean (none). But anyway...

Pineapple is the starter labour-inducer, the method you adopt when you're not really sure you want to go into labour, and you're still hoping that, between natural vaginal delivery and c-section, someone will discover a third way. For a start, you can eat it on your own (unlike curry, which you have to eat in tandem. It is actually less of a taboo to have a baby on your own than it is to have a vindaloo), which means you can do it all day. It also tastes nice, and I know this because sometimes you see people eating it who aren't even pregnant. Better still, it almost definitely doesn't work.

So I bought a pineapple, and C came home, and said, "What's this?" and I said, "It's a pineapple" and he said, "Why isn't it in a tin?" and I said, "Well, because then it would be in a tin", and he said "But that's so much more convenient. This doesn't even stand up on its own" and I said, "Babe..." The baby had not yet been born, so I was still calling him Babe. I soon adopted the alternative, Horse's Arse, and I must admit this was not principally to distinguish him from the baby. "...when did that turn into a house rule? The baby won't be able to stand up on its own", and he said, "Yes, but there are units of baby storage that take that into account", and I said "Well, I don't need to store the bloody thing. I'm going to eat it", and he said, "All of it? Does that mean I have to stay home from work?" and I said a number of things, clustered round the theme that, by the tone of his voice, he obviously thought staying home from work was worse than having to have a baby.

So that put him right off the second idea, which is to have sex.

Third is the raspberry leaf tea, but I didn't want to try this because I was still thinking of it as the nuclear option, having met a woman at a party who had a cup to celebrate her last day of work and then went into labour on the tube home. At this stage, the ripe old age of 34, I had still not realised that some people at parties talk bollocks.

Fourth is the above-named curry, but I was trying to avoid that because my sister shared one with her husband, the night before she had her first daughter, and then found the smell of his breath so revolting that while she was in labour I had to leave work, go and buy him some Listerine and then deliver it to the hospital, and I'm not even exaggerating.

Fifth is physical jerks – walking up and down hills, doing high kicks, cleaning windows, that kind of thing.

You are probably thinking, "None of this sounds desperate at all. This just sounds like some unusual food combinations and a bit of coerced sex. This is no more desperate than a holiday in Morocco." I have saved the most desperate for last: you roll down your cervix like a turtle neck and you'll go into labour within the half hour. Some midwives swear by it, and others think that the ones who suggest it should be struck off. Ha, never mind that I can't remember which bit counts as your actual cervix – I can't even remember what a turtle neck looks like.

Oh, sorry, there's one other idea, which is to stop eating, and starve it out. It's like Fantastic Mr Fox, only with a foetus. It was suggested to me by my French nanny, who stopped eating one month before her due date, and had her son two weeks early. I tried it the second time around, and I can tell you nothing about its efficacy because on day one I was in McDonald's before the stroke of noon, gripping the counter and shouting, "I just want a fucking McFlurry!" I want to say everybody's appetite is different in their third trimester, but instead I am going to say that French people, and French women in particular, are lunatics.

There are always some women who, instead of giving you stupid, ineffective tips, will shrug and say, "It'll come when it's ready." And then there are others – often the same people, actually – who will say, "You worry about them a lot less when they're on the inside. When it comes out, you'll be wishing you could put it back". These two statements are the only ones that are true, and plus, they save you a lot of faffing about and eating things you don't want and badgering sex out of someone who would rather be checking his emails, or doing almost anything else. But it's impossible to listen because you are not yet ready to cede control to the imps of chance. You still think that, if there's something you want to do, even if you're not 100% sure you want to do it, there ought to be something you can do to at least set it in train. There isn't. Seriously, go back to bed.

The reason I'm so fatalistic is that I went into labour on my due date: if I'd gone nine days overdue, I would have a lot more to say about turtle necks and a lot less to say about things arriving when they're ready. All day long, it was definitely happening – it just wasn't that bad. I took the dog for a walk, went to KFC. C had a Zinger Burger; I remember thinking, what an impossibly selfish oaf to choose a delicious crunchy spicy coating when I've got indigestion and am also in labour. Went back home, watched Together, the Swedish film about how much you can screw your children up if you don't look after them properly.

It still didn't hurt that much, though 5% of me thought that maybe I was one of those women who don't really feel a lot of pain. It sounds ridiculous, but my mother insists that she never felt labour pains – it was more like the dull irritation of repetitively using the same muscle. She then furnished us with some statistic, in the region of 1%, for women who don't feel contractions. Of course I'm not an idiot: I knew she was making the maths up. But what we didn't piece together, my sister and I, till ages afterwards was that our mother had two planned caesareans. She didn't feel contractions because she never actually went into labour. She never even went near labour – we were both a month early. This is the kind of thing you have to contend with when you're pregnant. The people who aren't telling you horror stories are telling you confidence-boosting stories that are, unfortunately, entirely fabricated.

What I was trying to avoid was a five-day labour, which is what happens if you sit around like a marshmallow and don't jolly things along with activity. This is the obsession of the first-time labourer, that a long one is a really, really bad thing. And it's true that it's not particularly fun and it's hard to go about your normal business. You'd feel a bit discombobulated in the cinema, or else it would have to be an incredibly good film. But in fact if you're not in that much pain, it doesn't matter so long as you don't stay awake the entire time and get yourself into a stew. Ah-ha, but if you're freaking out about how long it's going to take, the exact thing you will do is stay awake the entire time and get into a stew.

So we arrive at hospital after 36 hours of this, surprisingly dilated (Six centimetres! Damn! I wanted to get through my entire story without using the words "dilated", "mucal" or "plug"), totally exhausted, ready for my marathon. I have a Tens machine, which is supposed to interfere with the neuro-transmitters responsible for pain, which I think it does by delivering massive electric shocks to your fingers whenever you forget it's there and try to fiddle about with it. The main reason I get into the pool, actually, is so I can take off the stupid thing without two midwives and a boyfriend telling me how surprisingly effective it is. Birthing pools, mean-while, are supposed to gate off your pain receptors. I'm not sure how: possibly they can't convey the messages "I'm wet" and "I'm in agony" at the same time, so they choose the most important message, and deliver that. (I cannot believe we got where we are today, as a species, by neurologically prioritising our wet/dry status over our perception of pain... I know I'm not Darwin, but still.).

Everyone quotes the Nice guidelines about birthing pools, which say they are "second only to epidurals" as pain relief options. This does not, by a million miles, mean what people intend it to mean, viz that it's like having an epidural, only one notch below. It means that epidurals work, and nothing else works, and of all the things that aren't an epidural, that have a very meagre, almost imperceptible impact on pain, birthing pools make a fraction more sense than chanting, or looking at a picture of your dog.

By now there is one midwife, a Glaswegian, I'd say in her fifties. In her favour: she has this amazing passion for Crime Scene Investigation. All of them, New York, Miami... the lot. She can't stop talking about it. It sounds like a small thing, but someone with an enthusiasm strikes me as more trustworthy than someone without one. Sure, unless it's for the BNP, or the circus. She also seems to me to be a leftie, from the way that she denigrates one of the consultants at the hospital, who wants to ringfence the rooms with views onto parliament for the private patients. (In fact I have been to a lecture by the consultant she was talking about, a senior anaesthetist with a clarity and speed of mind that would be dazzling, I like to think, even if you weren't pregnant. But once the midwife arranges this conversation for me along political lines, I am automatically on her side.)

Not in her favour (I'm back on the midwife): she keeps telling me about her own experience of childbirth, which took place in Cyprus, and where she was under the care of midwives whose "agenda" (she says) she disapproved of. Only she doesn't tell me what their agenda was, so I end up, just with my sympathetic noises, siding with her against the mistaken Cypriot midwives of yesteryear, when actually, I think, if I'd been given a fair and balanced précis of the facts, I would have sided with them. In Cyprus, you get drugs, is what I'm saying. This midwife is much more into water births (probably also chanting, positive visualisation, all those things that don't work). I stay in the pool for another four or five hours. About five minutes before the end of her shift, she reads my birthing notes aloud, which say, "I probably will want an epidural." She scoffs, and then her shift finishes. The next time I appear in this building with birthing notes, just under two years later, I have written: "I DEFINITELY want an epidural. I DO NOT want to give birth on a midwife-led unit. I AM NOT interested in alternative forms of pain relief". (A GP who read the Guardian has emailed me and told me what to say. How this ended is a story for another day.)

Anyway, CSI: Glasgow is replaced by a much younger midwife, with no enthusiasms, televisual or otherwise. I feel shortchanged. I must be pretty far gone by this time, because I remember seeing her sitting in the corner making notes on something – of course it must have been me, and my labour, she was taking notes on – and deciding that she was actually doing a crossword in a puzzle magazine. When we have an altercation later on, about whether or not my contractions were intermittent and surfable, like in the books, or constant and unbearable, like in real life, I finish with, "And you can stop doing your stupid puzzle!" And she says, gnomically, "Better out than in", as if I have a limited supply of raging misapprehension, and if I will just vent two or three more totally wrong accusations ("And you can give me back my toenail clippers! And you can tell your brother I do not want a lager and lime!"), then I'll be spent, and turn out to be a really nice lady.

Theoretically, you get to the phase of "transition", and feel a range of emotions. Who knows, you may run the gamut from horror to despair. Midwives always tell you funny stories about transition: "Well, one lady put her coat back on and said she wanted to go home! One asked for a divorce! Can you imagine?". This is classic obfuscation: probably there was one woman who wanted to go home, probably there are a load of divorces, but there is nothing cute or colourful or kooky about it – it is just plain, brutal pain. There are only two things that make it remarkable – first that it is so bad, and second, that anybody would expect anybody else to endure something so bad without analgesia.

All the way through the classes, you say, "So this epidural, then. How does that work? Why doesn't everyone have one?" I was told all of these things: a midwife said, "It can leave you paralysed, but that's quite rare – I think it's only one in 25,000." One in 25,000? Rather than rant about a typical midwife's grasp of statistics and manageable risk, never mind the unwritten Royal College of Midwives guidelines on Making Up Any Old Rubbish, I am going to quote from Anaesthesia UK, an educational site for anaesthesia professionals. "Permanent paralysis resulting from epidural analgesia during labour is so rare that clear figures on its incidence are not available. A recent review of 500,000 cases performed in the United Kingdom did not reveal a single case. One case has been reported in Australia. In this case, the patient had a rare malformation of blood vessels around the spinal cord. This was unknown to the patient and resulted in a blood clot which caused compression injury to the spinal cord." See what that says, in its sober way? It says, "This never happens." It happened once in Australia, which is the same thing. There is one recorded case of a death following an epidural, in the history of its use in the UK, and that was when someone tampered with the drug that was being administered. One is often told that it lengthens labour, without being told that a) 36 minutes in pain is longer by an almost infinite margin than

36 hours not in pain, b) that the average lengthening of labour is 22 minutes, and c) that the figures are opaque, long labours tending to exhaust women and make them more likely to ask for an epidural.

The other thing you're never told is that there's a pretty much global policy on epidurals, which I learnt from a) my own labour and b) all the novels I've ever read with a labour scene in them. They say, "See how you get on," and you think, "Right, getting on fine, check me out, I'm made of iron filings, oh… oh, *this* is what they were talking about. I need the drugs, I need the drugs right now", and then they say, "Oh, it's too late now – you'll have the baby in an hour." Always. Without fail. I do not understand it. I went to a lecture by an anaesthetist at St Tommy's, and said, "If there's no medical downside, why doesn't everybody just ask for an epidural as soon as they get in?" and she replied, "I suppose that's why you'd go private." It's just for the money, in other words. It makes my blood boil: it's not for the foetus, it's not for maternal health, it's not for anything but the money. I can think of no clearer outrage against women in the entire system of western medicine, that our physical distress is considered too workaday, too pedestrian, to be countered. When I hear any of the blarney surrounding this, from new-agey notions about how empowering it is to have an unassisted labour, to more traditional paternalism (a midwife named Denis Walsh opined in 2009 that women should go through the pain because it helps them "prepare for the responsibilities of nurturing a newborn baby"), it fills me with an indignation so powerful I could run a generator off myself.

But anyway, there I am. I've got out of the birthing pool, because things have stopped happening, and suddenly things start happening. Missy is doing her puzzle (in my imagination), C is looking, to give him credit, as distressed as I've ever seen him, I'm asking for an epidural but I'm all out of time. We switch rooms, so I can look at the Houses of Parliament from my pit of despair, and also so someone else can use the birthing pool, which I have dropped a bit of Kit Kat in. Then there's, like, an incredibly long 42 minutes…

yik yak yik yak…

nearly there…

lovely baby!

I remember looking round to see him on the mat: he looked incongruous, like a baby from a war zone suddenly landed in a municipal gym. They said he was a boy, and I shouted, "I can't believe it's a boy!", like I'd won the lottery. (Who knew I wanted one of those? I didn't.) And I can date that pretty accurately as my last moment of peace:

then I picked him up, and realised how much he meant to me, and now I'm just blancmange. A big, hairy, fearful, emotional heap of blancmange. Only now I've got two, so I'm twice as bad.

CHAPTER 5
Is breast best?

Or is it all just milk?

It's bliss. There you are, in a state of bliss. The baby smells like the bit at the end of Perfume (I have not read it, but I have seen the film), where the murderer has created a scent so intoxicatingly beautiful that, as he rises to be hanged, the crowd collapses before him in an orgy of love and the purest sensory fulfilment.

That is literally what my baby smelled like. One of my earliest worries for his safety was that someone might try to eat him. I think perhaps it would be considered patronising, so experts rarely spell out how much you're going to love your baby. They'll parcel it up in some supplementary bit of advice, like, "Mum might be exhilarated for the first couple of days, so, Dad, you've really got to step in on day three…" Some titbit of timetabling, and you think, "Huh, why would I be exhilarated? I'll just have given birth."

It's hormones, innit? It's accelerated love to make you look after them, while you go about falling in love with them, over time, in the proper way. But they are amazingly good hormones; I don't understand why nobody's tried to synthesise them for use recreationally.

No, people don't go on and on about this, not because it's obvious, but because, I imagine, if it doesn't happen you already feel bad enough without the full force of post-natal lore telling you how aberrant you are. Breastfeeding is slightly different: if it works, it is so obvious, so intuitive, so easy, so effective, so efficient and tidy, so emotional and fulfilling, so heartwarming, so incredibly beautiful, that the existence of a book on the topic is baffling to you. It would be like having a book called How to Breathe, or What to Do If You Don't Like Nature, or Your Guide to Appreciating Birdsong or Friendship or Sunlight. But it goes wrong all the time.

There will be people in the breastfeeding lobby baying for my blood over this, but you know what? I don't care. (This lobby is inexplicably powerful: it is more powerful than the tobacco lobby; witness, in my lifetime, in *my adult lifetime*, it has become unacceptable to smoke in a pub, yet acceptable to breastfeed. It's against the laws of the natural universe, in which a cigarette goes incredibly well with a pint, whereas a nursing baby does not really go that well with any drink apart from Ribena. Ten years ago, I was doing a little piece on breastfeeding in restaurants, and I rang some quality establishments to check their policy. The Wolseley in Piccadilly said, "Yes, of course you can breast-feed. But you can't bring a baby in here.")

Sorry. To get back to hospital, T was just this magic little chap – I think he worked out how to feed before he even realised how to get his eyes open. He ate all the time. That's what they do at the beginning, to get the colostrum out, since it is so incredibly full of goodness and yet not very substantial, and any baby who knows anything at all will be trying to get it out of the way, to bring the real milk in. Then, once the milk is in, they eat all the time, and this is called "cluster feeding", which is intended to establish supply – too much supply, if anything – so that they can relax and stop worrying about it. Once supply is established, they might carry on eating all the time, and now you have to admit that you just have one of those babies that eats all the time. C's parents came to see us in the hospital, on the second day, when I was just about to be discharged. They are Baptists (the denomination of Christianity – they're not qualified to get in early and baptise your baby), and the midwife, unaware of their faith status, tried to have a conversation with me and C about contraception before we left the building. Mr and Mrs C were appalled, though

I do not, at this juncture, think they still believed we were saving ourselves until we got married.

So anyway, we got home, me and tiny, delicious-smelling T sat on the sofa, and for about the next six months, on and off, me and Mrs C had this conversation: "Tuh! Are you feeding him, again? He can't be hungry again. He's only just eaten!" "I'm feeding on demand" "He didn't demand!" "I don't care." "Tuh! Are you *feeding* him? *Again?*"

Six days in, we all went for a walk, and T set up this minuscule, almost imperceptible mewl, only to me he sounded like he was trapped in a burning building. At the speed of Bruce Willis, I raced into the cafe on the common and bought some water; huffed and puffed at the waitress, to indicate how intolerably slow she was at punching numbers into a till; raced back to where C and Mrs C were standing, wondering where I'd got to; snatched T out of the pram, ripped my top off, prised apart my (for the record, a bit bondagey) nursing bra, and was feeding him, standing up, essentially naked, in October, in the park, while C and his mother – who, I think in common with many mother-son dyads, had never stood together watching a naked woman – stood, watching.

"Phew!" I turned around, beaming. "He's stopped crying. Isn't he good?" The scene was lent eccentricity by the fact that we weren't just anywhere in the park: we were right on the bandstand. So it looked a bit like I was doing performance art.

About five days later, exactly the same thing happened on the high street, though this time it was just me and T, so from the wider family's point of view it was much less embarrassing. Again, I ripped all my clothes off as if in a strip joint frequented by early man, but this time it didn't work as fast as normal, and T carried on crying. So I decided that perhaps my milk had run out, and checked (like it says in books) by squeezing my nipple – I'm still on the street, by the way – and accidentally squirted myself in the eye. Now I am blind, and also practically naked, and blocking the door to Woolworths, with a screaming baby.

I didn't need these examples. I could quite credibly have said I was never one of those women who could feed invisibly. It even sounds unlikely, doesn't it? Like "invisible mending" – except I have seen it done, the complex origami where a vest folds down and a T-shirt folds up, and the baby's head obscures everything else, perfectly, almost as if it were designed for this sort of thing. Of course I'm impressed. To pretend I wouldn't have preferred to be like this would be stupid – it would be like wishing you hadn't had your hair cut, or kept food off your clothes. I'm not, however, impressed by those giant bibs you see women wearing. The whole NCT group gathers into a coffee shop, and one by one, affixes huge plastic bibs, with a 1950s print of maybe cowboys or flowers... Two of them will have the same one, always. I don't know whether this constitutes a social faux pas, or whether the very fact of grown women donning bibs in a public space is cause enough for the suspension of normal rules.

But sure, the politics of breastfeeding in public are right. If you want to, then you should. I was being flippant about the cigarettes. The practicalities of it are variable, but the people who really want to do it, anywhere, while they're doing other things like shopping, generally get pretty good at it. I could never really luxuriate in it unless I was on my own. With T, I was always stunned by this amazing vantage point, being able to gaze at him, watching his changing face. Sometimes, when he was feeding, he used to clutch his head with his open hand, like he'd left his briefcase in a taxi; it was one of a gallery of dinky poses of which I should dearly have loved photographic record, but if anyone can come up with a way to get a picture of a breastfeeding baby without getting a great big breast in the way, then I will find a way to give that person a Nobel prize. With H, my second, there was all that, but also the peace. You get loads of peace with your first baby, and none at all with your second, because you're constantly feeling guilty about not giving enough attention to your first. So you get 20 minutes, on your own, when you can stare at the baby and nuclear-love her, and have a nice sit down at the same time. It is golden time. If I had to Desert Island Discs the minutes of my life, these would be my minutes.

You'd think, wouldn't you, that I would be the poster girl for breastfeeding, that I would love breastfeeding activists (or lactivists, as they like to be known – I'm actually not making this up) and they would love me. No, and for so many reasons, most of them personal. I personally did not keep it up long enough. I started giving T parsnip at around four and a half months. I know there are bits of parenthood that require more patience than feeding: terrible twos; adolescence; the years between 20 and 25 are apparently very hard. But seriously, it is no accident that whenever there is a depressing scene in a drama about an old people's home, it features some mashed food and a teaspoon. Anyway, I started that with T because I had a strident friend and she told me to. And when H was born, the advice was very clear that they shouldn't have solids until they're six months, but it ran so manifestly counter to the evidence of my own senses (she would mime chewing when the rest of us were eating, for instance – famished!) that I took no notice. They were both weaned off breast milk totally on their half-birthdays. T had gone off it, and would crane around the room looking for more interesting things, clearly unaware that he had a role to play in the preservation of my modesty. It was like going for a date in a pub with the football on. And H wasn't sleeping well, which I put down to the fact that breast milk only fills you up for about 36 minutes, indeed, from a satiation perspective is useless, is essentially water that tastes of booze and garlic.

Because I was writing a column about T for the Guardian at that point, I had quite a few emails to the effect that I had given up very soon, as it would have been better for baby if I'd stuck at it, and a load of new age stuff about how we're not adapted to cow's milk, any more than a dog would be adapted to goat's milk, and all of this I took very little notice of.

I began to take notice of the whole culture, though, when I read an article in the Atlantic magazine (www. theatlantic.com/doc/200904/case-against-breastfeeding) which, looking back, I think marked the beginning of the breastfeeding backlash.

The point is, if it works, it's great. If it works, it's the best thing on earth. But for plenty of people, and I mean loads, I mean at least half of everybody I know who's ever had a child, it does not work that well. Some of them couldn't get enough milk going, and actually never managed to; some had nipples that were too big, or a baby with a too-small mouth, or a baby with a tongue-tie, or a baby that just didn't feed, got jaundice from not feeding, had to go back into hospital and by the time it came out, was bottle-accomplished but no longer knew how to do it the old-fashioned way. Someone had appendicitis and had to go into hospital when her baby was 14 days old, hadn't had time to express; the baby was on formula for a week and then didn't want to switch back (formula looks nicer; it would surprise me in no way if it didn't also taste nicer). Some people got post-natal depression and had to stop breastfeeding to take the Prozac, some other people got an infection in their c-section scar and had to take antibiotics that weren't milk-friendly. Some other people were incredibly tired, and needed a break.

And I haven't even started on the problems that the books and leaflets actually admit – the mastitis, the fact that some people just find it incredibly painful. One friend went to a breastfeeding workshop where a mother said it hurt so much, she was setting her alarm to go off 40 minutes before the baby woke up, just so she could neck enough analgesics and have time for them to take effect before she started. And the midwife nodded, and said, "You're doing exactly the right thing." Another friend had thrush so badly, and was also so nuts, that she turned up at a workshop, just flopped her breast out of her clothes and shouted, "Look at it! Look at the colour of it! It's bright red", and a trio of health visitors flapped around her, trying to soothe her and tuck her back in at the same time.

I'm not saying these problems are insurmountable, rather that however timeless and bountiful the activity is, there is a vast assortment of things, medieval and modern, that can go wrong with it, and generally speaking, they are not the mother's fault. So if, as a matter of policy, you're going to persist with this orthodoxy that breastfeeding is the only acceptable option, that even a small amount of formula mix 'n' matching will destroy the protective qualities of breastmilk, then you need to have a bloody good case.

In fact, the case for breastfeeding is not that strong, and it has passed so seamlessly into the book of What's Best for Baby that it's often very lazily put. To give an example, there's a charity called Best Beginnings, which aims to foster breastfeeding confidence etc, and is endorsed by the Department of Health, the Health Protection Agency, the NHS... the full force of nationalised health provision. Its opening statement is, "Did you know that babies who aren't breastfed are five times more likely to end up in hospital with serious tummy bugs? Or that in countries like Australia or Norway, people think breastfeeding is as normal as putting the kettle on?" I asked them for the source for that first statement and they did not respond. (The second statement, I don't think anyone could source. I include it only because it is stupid.) I finally sourced it myself, and it comes from an article in Ecology magazine. Here's the thing: that figure is from the World Health Organisation, which presents it as a global collation of statistics. In other words, this is not comparing two babies from Surbiton. It's comparing breastfed babies to formula-fed babies from countries where they might not even have an assured water supply or sterilising equipment or electricity, where they might not even have enough formula. It's an absurd way to propagandise for breastfeeding. It's as good as lying. If they were flogging a Pot Noodle, they wouldn't get away with it.

Anyway, to be brief, it is emerging that breastfeeding definitely protects babies against gastric bugs, but only to the tune of four babies in 100 getting one less bout of a bug, over the period that they're breastfed. Since you can't tell the difference, at this age, between diarrhoea and a normal poo anyway, this doesn't seem like a claim you'd want to stake your reputation on. In the one intervention-ist study that has been done, there is a six-point spike in IQ among breastfed babies and, personally, that's good enough for me. And anyway, it is so brilliant when it works that I would have breastfed even if it had made the babies' IQ go down. But for all the rest, the evidence is much milder: the statistics showing less asthma, less eczema, less obesity, fewer ear infections: these haven't been adjusted for social class and environment. It boils down to, "Middle-class babies do better; middle-class babies tend to be breastfed." Babies, in this respect, have something in common with the rest of humanity, in that the more affluent they are, the better their general health; research suggests that this holds true until the wealth gap gets so extreme that everybody's prospects deteriorate. That's a whole different conversation, but it's notable, at every point in the business of gestation and baby-rearing, that the less interested the political process gets in meaningful socio-economic overhaul, the more interested all the parties become in the miniature details of individual behaviour that, not long ago, would have been considered nobody's concern but one's own.

As I write, we're coming up to a general election, and the Fatherhood Institute has just produced a briefing "on the benefits of paternal engagement", intended as a guide-line for government strategy. Among its advice comes this little nugget: "Fathers' beliefs that breastfeeding is bad for the breasts, makes breasts ugly and interferes with sex are associated with mothers' bottlefeeding intentions." Dads, huh? Where do they get all their ridiculous ideas? This is a lovely distillation of socio-medical orthodoxy, the way it expresses itself – first, take something that is self-evidently true (in its aftermath, breastfeeding makes your tits look like bananas in a Waitrose bag, and dead right, while you're doing it, it interferes with sex. I have just taken a look at my left breast. If I had one ounce, seriously, 28 grams less restraint, I would take a picture of it and post it on the internet. I don't want to whine, so I'm not going to describe it in detail; let's just say that if I found myself in the Amazon, and I wanted to join one of their world-famous ladies' archery tribes, ain't nobody'd be asking me to cut anything off).

Anyway, they take this truth, but subtly attribute it in such a way as to indicate that anyone who would think such a thing is either an idiot or totally unfeeling. They don't specify which, so they don't have to make their own case; they just have to make them sound bad, these callous, stupid dad-bastards. The word "associated" is an all-time favourite in almost-science, since it sounds like the kind of modest, thoughtful claim a credible statistician would make ("Oh no no, we would never say 'cause': we are much too scientific to be so bold…"). In fact, it is only an association, and it doesn't mean that much: a think tank, or a government green paper, or a white paper, or a clinical guideline has no place interceding in the sex lives of new parents. If that's the kind of show we're running, here, why not tell 18-year-olds that watching porn gives you a headache (sorry, that watching porn is "associated with getting a headache")?

My sister said this was a tacit World Health Organisation strategy to bring down the global population, since you can't get pregnant while you're nursing. Although actually you can, but never mind that. I thought, bollocks: it's just a pub argument, amplified to the level of policy, where the less evidence you've got, the noisier you are. But by chance, the NHS's Change for Life campaign recently brought out a leaflet, Start for Life, that gave the guideline of exclusive breastfeeding for six months. Or, as they put it: "Don't rush to mush… This is because babies are developing on the inside as well as the outside, and although we can't see it, it takes about six months for a baby's digestive system to work properly, and be able to cope well with solid food."

Now, this is strange, I thought. Surely, even to the underclass, even to the feral poor of Broken Britain, you don't need to explain that there are things happening inside the human body that you can't necessarily see? It continues: "Plus, if you feed them breastmilk up to and beyond six months it gives them even more protection against infections. Some baby foods may have 'from four months' on the label, but it's important to remember that this information is based on outdated research."

There's the rub: "new research". So I called the Department of Health, and asked to be directed to the "new research". Nothing for a week, then I called them back and a man said, "This is from the World Health Organisation." I said that wasn't good enough: the WHO is a global organisation, and advice for mothers in Honduras wasn't necessarily appropriate for mothers in the UK. Did they have their own new research? He referred me to a colleague, who accidentally copied me in on his email. "I told her to go to the WHO, but she wasn't having any of it," he said. "Can you put her off? She's quite feisty!"

I finally got the document they were referring to, which was a review of 22 studies, 11 from the developed world, 11 from the developing. It found the following:

1. Exclusive breastfeeding has a prophylactic effect against gastroenteritis. But this is pretty small in the developed world: as mentioned earlier, it amounts to four babies in 100 getting one fewer episode of diarrhoea, over the period that they're breastfed.

2. Breastfeeding contributes to maternal weight loss. It was actually two interventionist studies from Honduras that showed this link. I mean, you can see why, from a global perspective, with an obesity epidemic, this looks like a good idea, but if we knew, ladies, if we only knew that one of four reasons that we're told to breastfeed exclusively for six months was for our own waistlines, then I think we would take this decision into our own hands, would we not?

3. Breastfeeding provides "prolonged lactational amenorrhoea". Which means? Which means you don't get your periods back while you're doing it. That's *it*. This is not about existing babies – this is about contraception. My sister was right, which never happens. We're being fed this line for the sake of a population curve in places where they have no access to contraceptives!

4. The "weanlings dilemma" is the term given to paediatricians trying to balance the protective qualities of breastmilk against the fact that four-month-old babies need more nutrients. This overview found that they don't need more nutrients, that breastfeeding them exclusively beyond four months was not stunting them. It's not a brilliant reason for eschewing solid food, though, is it? "You're fine – you can survive on breastmilk." I could probably survive on Slim-Fast, but I don't want to.

It is, in short, a swizz. I understand it better from the WHO perspective, where they are trying to control fertility in very poor areas, where they have to look at obesity through the largest possible lens. But from the health service of a developed nation, it is a total swizz.

When H was two months old, T had this horrendous fall. I want to say he fell downstairs, but actually he fell off the stairs, because we had an open staircase, which every family member and friend to enter the house, since he was born, has told us to put banisters on. Gah, it was horrific, and not only was it our fault in any long-term blame assessment, I was also standing *right there* when he fell six feet (it's the equivalent of an adult falling 25 feet) and I still can't fathom what combination of physical incompetence and mental paralysis prevented my catching him or even seeing which bit of himself he landed on. You know in films, where crisis unearths amazing abilities in people, and they can suddenly run really fast or have brilliant reflexes? It appears that in some people, catastrophe produces the opposite effect. What a horrible realisation this is. I'm never going to save anybody, unless I am forewarned by two weeks. Even then, I will probably just flap.

Anyway, we all four of us went into casualty, but T had to stay in overnight. H was not that easy as a tiny baby – she got what the French call the blues of the night, which is just a romantic way of saying she screamed from five till midnight. So I took her home, left her with my mother, came back to hospital where the little man was crashed out and tiny-looking in his cage-like bed, and the nurse goes, "We do support breastfeeding mothers, you know."

"How do you mean?" I said, thinking: this is the *last* of my problems. I'm waiting for T to get a Cat-scan, to check he hasn't disastrously dislodged his upper vertebrae.

"You can bring the baby back in – we do support you in your breastfeeding."

I'm not having a rant about the nurse, who seemed like a kind person (nurses in children's wards, in my, thank God, slight experience, are the nicest people in the world); it just seemed so strange. All your thoughts are on your toddler, who could have seriously injured himself, and they're still on about the nutritional superiority of sodding breastmilk! Which they have totally overstated in the first place!

In the morning, I went back to fetch H and bring her back in, and for the whole day, whenever the meals came round, the nurses would holler, "There's a breastfeeding mother in there! Make sure you get a food order from the breastfeeding mother!" So of course I was also worried that anybody who hadn't seen the baby would think I was still breastfeeding the two-year-old. But it fosters a strange culture, between mothers and medics, and between mothers and other mothers: as the person doing the right thing, you get all this exaggerated approval from the people in charge, and other mothers will say things like "Well done" and "You're good", but the undertone is that you're a bit of a twat – something along the lines of, you're the fool who believed the headmistress when she said you had to wear a bobble hat, and now you're making everyone else look bad, and you're also standing there in a bobble hat.

Of course there's going to be a right way and a wrong way with feeding children. There are nutritional verities that apply to everyone. I'm not some thick contrarian on a mission to prove vegetables are bad for you. I just wonder whether this isn't causing more social fissures than it warrants.

Having said all that, I hate hate hate stopping. The first time I gave T a bottle – and we're not talking a bottle of Tropicana, here, or a martini, but my very own milk that I'd made earlier – I was so worried that some foreign, chokeable object could have slipped into it (like a pea, or a badge) that I thought I would pass out. (My sister said sagely, afterwards, "Anything as big as a pea or a badge wouldn't get through the teat.") When I decided to wean him, I had serious doubts about what it would do to our relationship – whether it would water down my ferocious love, or scramble his understanding of the world. With H, I didn't even express any milk. I didn't establish any amount of separation until she was quite a substantial wee thing, so that the first day I attempted to leave her with someone else and a bottle, I was upstairs, lying on the floor, in despair. Clutching my head, going "I'm in despair! Despair!" to nobody.

And then you've stopped, and it's all over, and you can't remember what all the fuss was about. It's like snapping out of a dream. What an incredibly weird, beautiful business. But I'll tell you what: when I look at mothers who didn't breastfeed their children, it never strikes me that they love them any less.

CHAPTER 6
Let me eat cake

The incredible human miracle
of food-related weight gain

Imagine you're a woman, right. Maybe you're 29 or 31. So you understand the facts of life, you get that pregnant people put on weight, but you haven't really given it the full force of your consideration. When my best friend's boyfriend was agitating to have children, one of her arguments for Not Yet was that she had only had a really flat stomach for about 17 months of her whole adult life, and she didn't want to spunk it up a wall for a stupid baby.

Well, I don't think she put it exactly like that.

I remember thinking how weird that was, though I didn't examine why I thought that until I was forced to by my own appalling assortment of enormous circumferences, a couple of years later. My assumption was based on a pretty simple, binary understanding of vanity, femininity, the human form. You're definitely going to put on weight while you have a baby; indeed, it is a fair part of your intention that it, ergo also you, will grow bigger. So how can you possibly care? How can you worry about what you're eating, what you look like, how you're holding up in relation to other pregnants? It's like boarding a plane to Malaysia and spending the whole journey worrying about your carbon footprint. Sure, it's not looking good, but it's only going to get worse. Maybe you should have reached an accommodation about this before you got on the hypothetical plane.

In fact, that's not how it works at all. You've spent your entire life, which, in the modern middle-class way, is not 19 years, it's nearly 35, aware of some key basics, viz eating all the time will make you fat, and being fat is not a desirable state of affairs, and here you are, eating all the time, getting fat. It is a state of constant torment. The fact that you are pregnant doesn't make it better at all. If anything, it makes it worse, because you can't even go to bed at night kidding yourself that the next day will be different. The next day will just be worse: you will be hungrier still and even fewer of your clothes will do up.

There's always someone who will say something to give you heart. Like, a person with morning sickness will get away with quite a lean first trimester because she feels too sick to eat much. That's all bollocks, by the way: quite often morning sickness makes you even fatter because all you can eat is ready salted crisps. But if you don't get it (I didn't get it), you just end up resenting the people who do for their easily managed appetites. One day, at about eight weeks pregnant, I guesstimated all the calories I would have not eaten, had I had even a small amount of nausea. I did it really carefully, counting only the things I'd eaten in the mornings, replacing them in my computation not with nothing at all, just with smaller, less calorific items. What an absurd use of my time. My finger is hovering over delete … I really don't want to look that petty-minded. But I am. Thirty-nine thousand calories, by the way. In eight weeks, that's what I could have saved myself just in the morning.

The galling thing is, I've never been that hung up on this women's magazine thin thing. I never had a flat stomach to start off with. I always bought the line that thinness is nothing to do with sex – it's about thin women wanting to dominate other, fatter women. I honestly believe that – I'm not just trying to sound like a third-wave feminist (although I am, also, a third-wave feminist). But there is a difference between not being hung up about it, and not wanting to be reduced to an ape-like state of perpetual hunger.

Anyway, the first six weeks are the most insane, I think. You know that line where an old man says losing your sex drive is like no longer being handcuffed to a psychopath?

This was like being handcuffed to 10 six-year-olds, on a birthday outing. A constantly warring cacophony of appetites, all a variation on absolute crap. I want an ice-cream. No, a doughnut! One doughnut won't be enough; I wonder if I can find a smaller one, then I'll be able to have five. Look, there's a Greggs over there; I haven't been in a Greggs for years! (Why not? Because this is heart attack food, this is a one-stop shop to a size 22). I wonder what Totten-ham cake tastes like. It seems rude not to try. (It will taste like a huge slab of cake, with pink icing. You idiot, just look at it.) You've got to hand it to McDonald's – it is incredibly good value (oh, the laughable self-deception. Like you're getting four cheeseburgers because they're only 99p each). At least if I went to Nando's I could overeat and yet stay Atkins (well, sure, if you hadn't just come out of McDonald's).

I want to say that the more I gave myself a hard time over it, the more I ate, but that isn't true. When I endeav-oured to forget all about it, had a serious word with myself in which I insisted that this too would pass etc, while I was having this interior dialogue designed to soothe the raging furnace of my appetite, I popped half a kilogram (*half a kilogram!* Do you have any idea how much energy that is?) of dates into my mouth without even noticing. In 11 weeks, before I even had a scan or was allowed to tell anybody, I'd put on a stone. I'd read the odd pregnancy-fashion tip ("Well into your second trimester, you'll probably still be in your jeans, but you might start to have trouble doing them up!") and I would want to be sick, though the sensation was nothing that a pack of ready salted crisps couldn't see off.

In retrospect, English obstetrics is pretty reasonable about weight gain in pregnancy. They never weigh you in your midwives' appointments, which is standard in much of Europe. You don't have a limit to how much you're supposed to put on (in France, they will try to shunt you towards a low-fat diet if they think you're getting too fat, which I think is anything over a stone and a half). I read a couple of things that made me furious (the agony doctor in the Observer said that anything more than 20lb would interfere with labour. Fool! I was fuming), but actually, people at the coal face of the baby industry were incredibly understanding about it. I only ever heard the most discreet remark, here and there, about how pregnant ladies should keep active with calming walks, and how if you got truly gargantuan, they might have a job guessing where to stick the needle for your epidural.

But it doesn't help. I wish the midwives had given me a harder time – that way at least I would have had a human being to fume at. I wouldn't still be on about stupid Googled advice from the bloody media doctor on a Sunday paper.

That's all I remember, from the whole thing: cake, fury and not being able to do my clothes up. Imagine, then, that you're out of your clothes, not in the regulation 20 weeks, but in six weeks. You don't want to buy maternity clothes yet. The shame, the defeat: it would be like buying incontinence pads on your 50th birthday. So you go out and buy something in the region of your original wardrobe, except two sizes bigger and, because you're intending this to be temporary, 70% cheaper. Ah, that's better. Now you look like yourself, except much fatter and much cheaper. This is absolutely disastrous. For about the next 15 weeks, you can barely leave the house: to catch sight of yourself in a darkened window would pitch you into a despond. Finally, you reach the point where it would be reasonable to buy maternity garments and, as you have looked so crap for so long now, pretty much anything will do. I must have spent three months in an oatmeal cardigan and "carpenter" maternity jeans, so called I think because I looked like the indolent git on a building site who could only do carpentry and was allowed to have five pints every lunchtime because he didn't do the heavy lifting. I had a pre-pregnancy skirt that (naturally) wouldn't do up, but I decided was fine for supermarket wear, and one time a lady in Sainsbury's ran up behind me and hitched it up. In my second pregnancy, I retreated totally into one dress, which I then couldn't wash unless I wanted to spend the day naked, so I looked and smelled like one of those kids with a really grubby security blanket, except I was wearing it. At what point does it go from fashion *erreur* to a mental health concern? The whole thing was totally catastrophic.

I wasn't blessed with morning sickness, but I did get hideous indigestion, which I thought might at least put the brakes on all the eating. And it did: it put the brakes on eating anything fresh. Finally, I thought, instead of just eating whatever it is I've eaten, and complaining about the indigestion for the rest of the day, I am going to make a list that goes Yes, No and Test. And it went: No: melon, grapes, oranges, bananas, apples, blueberries, strawberries, *all fruit*. Onions, garlic, mange-tout, yellow pepper, lentils, parsley, basil, spinach, lettuce, courgettes, *all vegetables*. All herbs. Test: potatoes. Yes: cake.

Though I did have really nice hair and fingernails. So that's something. And I have a friend who got such a ferocious appetite when the baby was born and she started breastfeeding that, by the second month, she could no longer fit into her maternity jeans.

The boyfriend of my abovementioned friend explained to both of us, way before either of us got pregnant, how it tends to work with breastfeeding – you lose the initial weight faster, and the first two weeks go very well for you.

But then you plateau, because the increased calorie demands are compensated by the huge amounts of food you fill your fat face with, and you can't then lose the weight until after the baby's weaned. I can't remember what his stated intent was in telling us this, but I got the distinct impression of a playful malice, a happy, "This is what you've got to look forward to, laydeez! I, conversely, shall retain my boyish form well into middle age!" "Ah-ha, the joke's on you," I thought, "because *I* won't be like that. I will be one of those women like Posh Spice, who undergoes some curious physiological reaction, whereby the more she eats, the more milk she generates, and the thinner she gets. It's going to be the best thing that's ever happened to me, procreating. I'm going to come out of it like a phoenix, with a cute little baby phoenix."

Ah, Posh. So much to answer for.

I don't know if you remember the singer/consort from her pre-children, pre-Beckham days, but she was like a normal girl. Not wildly attractive, but not at all fat. She just looked more like a 1990s famous person than a noughties one. She had Brooklyn, her first child, and around this time it became de rigueur for magazines to have "Wow! Isn't she thin?" covers every week. Just as an aside, what an amazing moment of realisation this was for journalism – there is almost no point on the weight-loss continuum that doesn't hint at an underlying drama, from messy break up, through new modelling contract, possible eating disorder, thyroid problem, all the way to cancer. All that, plus nice, thin pictures. I am amazed it took until 1999 for this to come together, but it did, and Posh's thinness was continually remarked upon, this despite the fact that there was not much going on with her own career (the band Spice Girls, you may or may not recall), and it was still (oh heady days) considered unfeminist to go on and on about the wives and girlfriends of footballers.

Anyway, called upon to explain her new physique, Posh said it was breastfeeding, and her mother was the exact same way. Look, I'm sure it's true, and even if it isn't, I don't care. I mention it only because I bought this hook, line and sinker, and so did everybody else. You talk to anyone who hasn't had children, or fraternised closely, like been married to someone who's had children, and they'll all go, "It's fine, isn't it? Won't you lose loads of weight breast-feeding?" How has it never occurred to any of us that perhaps Posh Spice was overstating her case slightly? Why do none of us wonder how it is that the world is not full of incredibly gaunt breastfeeding mothers? Does it not strike you as puzzling, when you see great herds of new parents running across the park doing buggy aerobics? Surely, if all you need to do is breastfeed, they should be in Starbucks, wondering what muffin to have with their frappuccino? Christ, where did the social convention even come from, that women lose their looks after they have children? Did it come from the miracle of lactation-fuelled weight loss? Or did it come from the fact that most people – well, no, a lot of people, well, no, me, let's just stick with me – put on three stone, both times, of which the baby and all its paraphernalia accounted for only one.

Breastfeeding takes about 500 calories a day, you are constantly informed, in a last-ditch attempt by health agencies to mop up those mothers who don't care about its (made-up) protection against ear infections. Hell, you're trying to feed a whole other person; maybe in a time of famine you would have to manufacture milk from your own fat stores, but in a time of plenty, your body helpfully reacts by fancying a Mars bar *all the time*. Do you have any idea how easy it is to neck 500 calories, when you're really hungry? Man, you can pop it into your mouth while you're deciding what snack to have before dinner.

In the third trimester, everybody around you starts to relax, and you can't work out why, and then you realise it's because you are now definitely pregnant. Before that, the whole world is a cat on the hot tin roof of your pregger temper. Strangers are too scared to offer you a seat in case you're just fat; friends are too scared to ask when you're due, in case you've already told them four times (which you have) and will take offence (which you will). I never got particularly worked up about that classic pregnancy bête noire, the pat on the stomach from the person who doesn't know you well enough, but I managed to wring umbrage from almost everything else. Broadly (and that's the word for it) three things happen: some people will just openly call you huge, to your face. My stepmother loved this. I have actually never seen her happier than when my sister and I were both pregnant, and she could trill around the house, "Look at you! You're enormous! Oh, look, there's another one… You can't miss her – she's a giant." She was like a creature of myth, of fairytale: a witch's cat had had her tongue for the past 190 years, and suddenly the spell was lifted. She could shout it from the rooftops: *"Check out your fat arse!"*

OK, so that's one approach. She was pretty extreme, but C wasn't far off. We'd go out to a person's house, and some nice acquaintance would say, "You don't look eight months pregnant", which is just a kind, meaningless thing you say to a pregnant. You don't expect her to make anything of it – you're just cheering her up. And he'd go, "No, no, but have you seen her from the side? Look how much bigger she is than the fridge!" He also had a side order of smartarsery, so I'd be standing at a mirror bitching and moaning at my horrible arse in my disgusting trousers, and he'd say: "Did you expect to do a whole pregnancy without putting on any weight?"

There's another type, and I've got to say I don't get this at all: people who want to call you huge, but are just marginally too scared or tactful, so they say oblique things to indicate that you're huge, while smirking. They might say a thing like, "You're looking a bit hot and bothered", and then, just in case you haven't clocked that that's an insult, their lips will quiver and they will hide under their polo neck. Or, my friend A said, "You look like Henry VIII", while I was having a brie sandwich. What can you say to that? "Are you calling me fat? Or greedy? Which is it?" Why, neither. Of course not. He was calling me *regal*.

There are plenty of people who simply don't understand why you would care, just as I never used to understand, just as maybe you don't understand – it's just life, why mind? I don't have any lingering resentments against these people, but I remember thinking at the time, "Why don't you just try to imagine why I mind, buddy? Walk a mile in my Birkenstocks, which, even though they are Birkenstocks, I have to wedge my pudgy feet into like I'm trying to plug a leak." (I didn't even have pre-eclampsia, by the way. Imagine how much more toxic I would have been with a condition whose major symptom is being angry.)

You always have a pregnancy celebrity-twin: it's even more exact now that gestation is such prime gossip meat. In the old days, you would maybe have heard on Radio 2 that, I don't know, Davina McCall was pregnant, but it wouldn't come up again until she appeared somewhere seven months in, and everybody said, "Doesn't she look lovely?" and that was that. Now, you will get due dates and symptoms; you might get a picture of the 12-week scan. So even if you don't get pregnant on a really clichéd day (like New Year's Eve or August bank holiday), you will still find a famous person exactly as pregnant as you. I got Charlotte Church. Then I spent the next six months looking at pictures of her, wondering whether she looked better than me, worse than me or about the same. It's ridiculous! She's 15 years younger than me, never mind one of the international super-rich, never mind hitched to a sporting personality! It would be like seeing a pregnant racehorse, and then moaning that it was going much faster than you, and had a much more luxurious coat, even though you were exactly the same amount of pregnant, with figures adjusted, naturally, for the fact that you're a lady and she's a horse. Just rank idiocy.

I only mention it because I remember telling a friend, when I was about three weeks off, that Church was my celebrity pregnant twin, and the tone in which she said "Really?" made me realise there was a further category: people who think you look ridiculous, who are even worried for you, because of how ridiculous you look, but you will see them in hell before they will give that away in word, deed, look or gesture. (Talking of celebrities, that is the other mistake – you think, well if famous people have the nubbins not to get fat, then it must be possible. I can't believe Madonna has more steel than me, you think. This is fallacious – those ones who look skinny with a bump, like a varicose vein, are the one who come out of their houses, or they're fictional ladies from sitcoms, in pregnancy suits. The ones who get fat stay indoors. In the 1950s primary school teachers had to give up work upon conceiving, because they'd remind children of sex. Now starlets who get pregnant have to give up work because they'd remind children of fat.)

So in summary, when I said people relaxed around you, in your third trimester, the other half of that sentence is, "...they shouldn't." This is the last time on earth for your cohorts to relax.

Funnily enough, my second pregnancy was slightly different because I didn't find out till I was 18 weeks, so some of the marathon eating, which must have been psychosomatic, didn't occur (though I do remember feeding T, in front of my cousin, and her saying mildly, "I never got into that, eating their leftovers". Leftovers, hah! I was lying underneath his high chair with my mouth open). Anyway, it was a very subtle difference, invisible to the naked eye, but I was slightly less huge with H, and when I got to about 36 weeks, people – attempting to be nice, I'm sure – started to say, "You're not as big this time." You'd think I'd be glad. I remember my second-time pregnant friend saying, "If I had a fiver for everybody who's said I'm bigger this time, I'd have *forty-five pounds*," and her lips were white with rage. But actually, it just made me worried that the baby wasn't growing properly. So all the old clichés are true: you can't have an opinion either way, can't stay without one, can't say anything and can't stay silent. There is definitely something to be said for dropping your pregnant friends, then picking them back up when they have the baby, relying on the likelihood that they will be so happy to have a baby, they'll forget you dropped them.

Some final thoughts on the entire aesthetics of pregnancy. No, of course I'm not talking about how pregnancy is represented in art or mainstream media. I mean your arse in pregnancy: some final thoughts on your arse.

Definitely don't do what I did and buy an extra, interim wardrobe; perhaps I'm reiterating, but I never spent a worse 200 quid in my life, and I'm including casinos. But nor do I agree with the Mumsnet line, which is to go into maternity shops, try on clothes and, if they suit you, buy them. It's not quite so demoralising (they tend to have really good lighting, or else no mirrors), but it's still a waste of money. Just wait till someone the same size as you gives you a big bag of stuff. What's the matter with you? Make a mother-friend. You're going to have to once you have a baby, anyway.

There is no vanquishing a pregnant or, for that matter, breastfeeding appetite. Don't barter with it – just give in. There will always be an annoying midwife, or book, or passer-by, telling you to think of the baby before you have an ice cream instead of a beautiful green salad. But actually, the link between foetal health and maternal nutrition is pretty shaky. And also, you can always make room for an ice cream *and* a salad.

If you're wondering how fast it all goes back to normal, well, I cannot speak for people who have willpower. I cannot speak for people who are 19. Naturally I cannot speak for Posh Spice. But this is what I found: for maybe a month afterwards, I had a pot belly, but I thought it was cute, for some reason, I thought it was like a badge of honour. Hormonal lunacy.

Then, about three months in, I didn't look quite so physically strange, but I caught sight of myself in the mirror; mismatched tops on a grey spectrum, a bit haggard, lank, random hair... I wasn't fat, but I wasn't thin and I looked just like Paul Weller. I said to C, "Do you think I sometimes look a bit like Paul Weller?", and he said, "You look nothing like him", but don't get him wrong, not in a reassuring way, more like, "Dream on, girlfriend".

Then, six months in, I still looked a bit like Paul Weller.

And then, suddenly, about three weeks after I'd stopped breastfeeding, it all went back to normal. No, of course it didn't just spring back, but one day, there you are, pretty much yourself, looking like maybe you've been living it up for a fortnight and are carrying a little holiday weight. All that fuss, you think. All that fuss, and I could have just waited it out, with a book in one hand and a custard slice in the other.

CHAPTER 7
What would Gina Ford do?

Hugging, smacking, drugging
and other things you should never
do to a childcare expert

When my sister and I were about 16 and a half months pregnant (in aggregate), our mother moved into the dead centre of London, which I think is functionally the furthest away she could have moved without it looking as if she was doing it on purpose. That has no bearing at all on what happened on her birthday; I just mention it to make her look bad.

So anyway, it was her birthday and we all went round. The babies (my one, T, and my niece, D) were about three months each, and that's when D had the longest, though apparently not the loudest, yell of her life. I thought screaming the place down was just an expression until I saw this: the flat was in a prematurely crumbling block, and for a while it looked like she might do it. T was never like that. My sister's oldest was never like that, either. Firstborns never are like that, apart from the ones that are, and then the second born is a whole different potato (although when a firstborn is like this, it quite often ends up an only child). Anyway, this is when my sister went Gina Ford.

Of course you've heard of Ford, but it tells you a lot about a person's agenda to hear them describe her in précis. Standard form is "parenting expert", but people who like her favour "baby guru" (or "miracle worker", or "magician", or – if you want to go a bit literary, "baby whisperer"). People who don't like her call her "the childless parenting expert", or "the self-help writer" or "that woman who makes babies sleep in coffins". I genuinely don't have a view, here – it never came up with T because I never wanted to put him down. First-time mothers who won't put their babies down are always called over-anxious, but it's not because we're anxious, it's because they're cute and we don't want to, *claro*? To us, that is like going all the way to a petting zoo in Devon, waiting nine months to get your hands on the cutest piglet in the south-west of England, and then someone going, "Are you never going to put that piglet down?" Nope. No, matey, I'm not. So, certainly with T, I was a "hugger mother", which is what media psychologists call people who don't go Gina (those who do are "scheduler mothers"). However, unlike many hugger mothers, I don't think Gina mothers love their children less than I loved mine: I think either their children are more highly strung than mine, or they have two or more children, or (God help them, this probably is the case), both. I never stop wanting to remark on how judgmental parents are, how the choices of anyone else, unless they are exactly the same as one's own, are considered an affront. Yeah, yeah, of course now *I* sound like I'm judging the entire state of parenthood. But I'm not. I'm a reasonable person, I like to live and let live. If you want to Gina, you go, girl. You Gina for your life.

It may help, or maybe it doesn't, that I've never read Ford's Contented Little Baby Book. What follows is more like a listening comprehension of all the conversations I've heard about it. If you're looking for real advice about a real baby, I suggest you go straight to the book itself. In the meantime, its thesis is that babies only get upset when they're tired or they're hungry, and if you were to regiment these stimuli a bit, feeding and putting them down at precise and predictable times, they would never get tired, and they would never get hungry. Hence the fabled contentment. There is an unscientific swarm of maternal opinion that just says, sod that, I would rather give it a cuddle. There is a slightly more vocal, though still broadly unsubstantiated thread you find a lot on Mumsnet that blames Gina for everything, from post-natal depression through to babies who grow up to be psychopaths.

There's a joint British/Danish study of hugger mothers versus schedulers (St James-Roberts, I et al, 2006, Pediatrics, 117(6), pp e1146-55), which finds that babies who get hugged all the time seem to be happier. At three ages when studied – 10 days old, five weeks and three months – the babies with scheduler mothers spent 50% more time fussing or crying. For example, at five weeks, the scheduler babies fussed/cried for 121 minutes of the 24 hours, compared with 82 minutes for the hugger babies. But I'm very sceptical, not about the research itself, but about attempting to draw practical conclusions from it. To get anything substantial, you'd need to know that crying and fussing was a bad thing. You'd have to know, furthermore, that there wasn't some kind of link between the kind of person who likes to schedule their baby, and the kind of person who takes things pretty seriously and might, themselves, cry and fuss 50% more of the time than the kind of people who hug. You'd need to know whether hugging and scheduling were learnt behaviours, or in the blood. I'm not saying you can't find this stuff out – possibly you can. But you've got to at least own your ignorance. A lot of people only schedule in the first place because their baby is a nutter who likes to scream the place down.

Which brings us back to baby D, who I used to call Angry D until my sister, in a brutish show of determination against self-evident truth, told me to stop it. S never bothered with the Gina method on feeding, but she did start the snoozes – one at 9.15am, one at lunch, one at teatime – and the result was a kind of miracle. Never mind that the child was now asleep for three of its 12 "waking" hours, which was an immediate improvement in 25% of life. She also spent the surrounding hours in a much better mood. She became incredibly good at going to sleep, so all you had to do was wrap her up, stick a dummy in and place her on a soft surface at the appointed juncture, and wham, she was asleep. It was like having a Tamagotchi. I went immediately from smug to jealous. I still had the more relaxed baby, but S had the baby you could rely upon utterly to be asleep. She could schedule herself a massive two hour me-time in the middle of the day. She could have done anything, taken an MA in maths, had an affair, brushed her teeth. Lunchtime was her oyster. T didn't start this until he was about seven or eight months old, and although he took eventually to it, his nap was never quite the banker that D's was.

And yet, here they are now, at two and a half, and their habits are pretty much the same. They're the same, also, in the fact that neither is 100% reliable any more, and it's not even going to last very much longer – they'll soon be staying awake all day. Then they'll go to school, and we'll have whole days of me-time, which we'll have to use for work.

They're pretty much the same children they started as. T is more relaxed but less biddable. No, D is not biddable, but when you bid her to do something, she is at least listening, and she definitely understands what you want, even while she doesn't intend to do it. My point is, it doesn't matter what you do: this could be the most contested area in all mothering, to hug or to schedule, and I'm afraid the true answer is that it doesn't make any sodding difference. There are easy babies and difficult babies, and different ones respond to different things and then, before you know it, they are no longer babies. If only there were some way to get all the time that all the people who've ever had this argument had spent on it: recover it, like with a hard drive; use it for something else, like world peace…

I do have one area in which I think there's a right and a wrong, and that's hitting children. I can't conceive of a situation in which hitting them would be the best course of action. There's been a very slight resurgence in this, the odd parenting contrarian who shoots straight to the fore of the media conversation, now that the not-hitting orthodoxy has gathered so much pace it's practically the law. Hitters, you notice, always say "smacking"; it sounds more benign than "hitting", which sounds more like domestic violence, or a pub brawl that ends in prison. And yet it is exactly the same action. I always try to insist on the adult terminology. Anyway, whenever they explain themselves, try to break through the crust of liberal rectitude with a bit of straight talking, it's always with an anecdote about when their four-year-old ran in front of a car, or stuck his finger in a plug. I've noticed (my sample is pretty small – maybe four media child-hitters) that this danger event is always played to maximum drama, so you get loads of, "I saw the flash of his blue trainers and he was out of the door, dashing towards the M1…" The aim is to exhilarate you so much with narrative pace that you forget your critical judgment. It never works on me, although maybe this is because I did in fact get run over, when I was five. It's not that exciting.

Anyway, back to danger-child. "Did I smack him/her? You're damn right I did! I don't think it did him/her any harm. I think it did a lot more good than reasoning…" My main problem with this is that they never describe it as an action they thought through. They're never painting a picture of an adult in charge, whose behaviour you might want to emulate, even if you don't like the idea of it very much. Rather, they describe an adult hysterical with anxiety and shock, behaving according to their atavistic instincts. So I always think, they just have poor impulse control. No big deal – we all have poor impulse control sometimes. But imagine trying to persuade the rest of the world that they, too, should control their impulses poorly.

Anyway, that's it, that's the limit of my binary parenting. I'd be thick if I didn't notice the trigger issues, though, the big divisions that set one parent against another. The less factual basis these arguments have, the more passion they command. It's a bit like the first world war. I'm sure there's some way of spinning cash out of this, maybe a live event that's somewhere between a freak show and a circus, where parents can mud-duel over totally unprovable propositions.

With vaccination, the fault lines are these: a loose collection of parents, ranging from hippies (who don't like "poisons") through to Daily Mail readers who are just disaster junkies, are against vaccination altogether. Their opponents are, naturally, very pro-vaccination, but also vehemently anti this rag-bag, on the basis that you need herd immunisation, otherwise it doesn't work. Sure, that's what they say; in fact they are just violently opposed to people, in this most precious arena of child-rearing, who don't agree with them, but this is one of those intoxicating instances where you are allowed to hate your opponents because they are physically, scientifically imperilling you and your offspring. Oh, suck it in, the righteousness! It's delicious, it's like a canister of oxygen after a month in Mexico City.

I am pro-vaccination, but I hate having my children vaccinated, to the point that H is five months late for her 12-week jabs, and T is 32 weeks late for his second MMR. I am the only parent in the western world to openly hold this position, even though I actually represent almost everybody. When I go in to get them jabbed, I make up the most elaborate excuses for my lateness – I moved to Italy, where they don't do vaccines; or he has had a cold for 17 weeks, and I didn't want to cross-infect him; or I have cancer – and the nurses wave me off, with this expression on their faces that nakedly says, "Enough! I can cope with the threat to herd immunisation, but I cannot cope with one more lame excuse."

Their first jabs, I always did on time. With T I didn't realise how awful it was going to be (so they'll take my precious, my beloved, the wellspring of all my joy, and they'll stab him in the leg... How bad can it be? Really?). With H, I had, unaccountably, forgotten how awful it was. I took T in, the nurse stabbed him with a huge needle and then said, rather blithely, like she was a mechanic waiting for a wheel to stop spinning, "Let's just wait till he stops crying and do the other leg, shall we?"

It took for ever. We were just sitting there, staring at him, while he showed no signs of ever abating, and I was pretty much crying by this point as well. What was she trying to inoculate us against – human pain? "Ooh, they don't normally cry this long," she said, and then, "Look at that – he's gone bright red! They don't normally go bright red!" It was an effort of tremendous will not to walk out before she'd finished, but I didn't. So we got home, both legs done, wholly immunised for the time being, I opened the door, picked up the post and found we were booked into the TB clinic the week after.

It was too much. They do all the babies from the same postcode on the same morning, so it sounds like an abattoir, apparently. I did not want to take T to the baby abattoir on a Saturday morning. My sister's midwife said it was because of all the foreigners in the area: they had to step up immu-nisations because they weren't routine in the immigrants' home countries. I wished she hadn't said this. I didn't want to be a racist refusnik; I wanted to be a coward refusnik. There's a difference. In the end, I got round it by going with C and T, stepping right into the room with them, leaving when the needle came out, going to be sick and then rejoin-ing my loved ones when they were finished. Amazingly, this was even worse than taking T in myself. It took much longer than I remembered it (nine and a half minutes), so I logi-cally assumed that he'd had a reaction and died.

My mother promised to do the 12-week ones, but when it actually came to it, she had tickets the whole month for the London International Mime Festival. I suppose it stands to reason that, when you've chosen someone to husband your screaming baby through injections because they are quite deaf, the odds are they might also like mime. C did those on his own.

So all we had left at this point was 16 weeks, 12 months, MMR and the pre-school boosters. If we can just get through the next two, I suggested to C, they will probably find a way to do the MMR with herbs by 2010, and then before he's five we can move to Honduras.

What hell. What hell on toast. And then you have another one, and have to do the whole thing all over again.

It feels like the past 10 years have been given over to establishing which idiot doctor's fault it was for the MMR vaccine to be associated with autism. Clearly, it finished up so far from the truth that it approached a hoax, and obviously Dr Andrew Wakefield isn't the doctor you'd get to do you a character reference, but at the same time, how much of this wasn't really about autism? How much of it was an excuse not to go for the vaccination? Come on, admit it, you feeble heaps. Injecting babies is the worst thing in the world. I would do anything to avoid doing their jabs. If Ronald McDonald told me vitamin K was unnecessary, I would find a way to believe him.

*

I met a woman once who I suppose you'd call the ideal mother. She had had her children very young, at 23, not because she had poor life prospects – far from it – but because she wanted children. She stayed at home to look after them, not because she couldn't get a job – she had a degree from Cambridge – but because she felt that it was best. Affluent, stable, slender, morally certain, apparently kind (I didn't meet her for very long), she was the mother that, underneath its ceaseless hectoring, the rightwing media is willing us all to be. She was also a modern impossibility, really; but she existed, so she'd probably dispute that. Anyway, I only sketch her because I thought she'd be above the phenomenon I'm about to describe. But no: she insisted, *swore* to me that there were some mothers who gave their children Calpol just to get them to sleep at night. I don't believe this, and I said so to a table of friends, and one said, "No, there *are*, there definitely are…" So I said, "Who? Anyone you know?" And she insisted, "Yes, someone I know", because it's difficult to back down at this stage of an argument, whereas making up somebody who does something is the easiest thing in the world. And yet I contend that even if there were people who did this, they wouldn't own up to it, unless they were talking to people to whom it was totally unremarkable. In short, not one of us knows anybody who has ever admitted to doing this.

It's a compelling myth, though, this parent who drugs for an easy life. I mean, apart from anything else, it's obviously bogus because Calpol just isn't that good. It's only a painkiller, not heroin. It's not even Medised. But there's a mental process when you drug your own child. The first time you do it is clouded with trauma. It's probably the only thing you've ever given them that isn't milk, so you are suffused with the sense that you're polluting their tiny form. If they don't seem to be all that ill, you're taking all this risk for nothing, and if they are running a temperature for the first time, you're really just Calpolling them so that when you arrive at A&E you look like you at least explored the options beforehand. It gets easier every subsequent time, but that in itself makes you feel like you've become blasé, that you've taken your eye (read, neurosis) off the ball. So the tension is, why am I putting myself through this gut-clenching hell? Or if it no longer clenches my gut, why doesn't it? Have I turned negligent? And wherever I fall on the spectrum of absurd anxiety, am I doing it for him or for me? Because he can't bloody talk, of course, so he might not even be in pain – he might be bright red and screaming just because he's angry, and he could be angry for any number of reasons. It is complicated further by the fact that the babyfather quite often has views of his own on Calpol; don't ask me why. You can get through almost all the hot potatoes of childrearing without the father ever proffering a view; avail yourself of one effort-saving drug product, and suddenly he's turned into a follower of the holistic principles of Ayurveda.

Anyway, I'm working up to a theory: Calpol-dosing is your classic parenting straw dog. I suspect myself of inadequacy or incompetence or selfishness – there's no way of proving or disproving that, I just have to place myself on a spectrum. So naturally, like any sensible person, I create an imaginary continuum on which there's a total sociopath at the end – a parent not just worse than me, but so much worse that I end up in the top 10%, I end up with an A* in parenting. They don't even wait till their child has a *temperature*. They're so desperate for bedtime, they have a measuring spoon in one hand and a corkscrew in the other, and that says it all about their relationship with children's analgesics. This isn't to be confused with the simple thrill of downward comparison, such as I experienced 20 minutes ago when I walked past someone who had failed to anticipate how wet puddles are when you really leap in them, and in consequence was wrestling a really loud, turbulent double buggy. That's just straightforward: there but for the grace of intelligence, foresight and properly fitted wellies go I.

These imaginary bad parents aren't three-dimensional "others", judged from a distance and found to be rubbish:

they are created out of my own deficiencies, they have no characteristics apart from to be worse, by the greatest credible factor, than I am. So one day they'll misuse Calpol, the next day maybe they'll just have the telly on for four hours (as opposed to my two).

Everybody does this, and everybody finds it on some level unsatisfactory because they know that this individual is a figment of their imagination. So we're constantly looking to one another for corroboration, which we provide just to be polite, to increase the net joy of social intercourse. This is amplified by a media that understands what we're after, and goes to the trouble of providing real-life examples of execrable parenting, which creatures they stalk to the ends of the earth like the last red squirrel of Scotland, then try to present as typical (or, tacitly, typical for a council estate). But the price we pay for being able to revel in real-life useless people is that we ourselves have to be without sin, so standards get ratcheted up and up, which is then reflected in policy, which brings us to the situation we're in now, where you have to pretend your child is two before you're allowed to buy Calpol, and to get Medised you have to pretend it's six. This is not easy at all when you have the child with you.

I never did this before I had children. Not once did I get into the office 20 minutes late and think, "I bet there are some people who have only just got out of bed." Or have a hangover and think, "Never mind that I wish I were dead; I bet there are some people who *are* dead! Who have literally drunk themselves to death!" Sure I felt inadequate, sometimes, but I never cared. I certainly never cared enough to create an underclass of incompetents to make myself feel better. So the difference, in parenting, is that you do care: you love the little bleeders, so it matters whether you're doing it right or not. That's the paradox: all this judgment of other parents, the suspicion and factionalism and often snobbery and prejudice, the righteousness, the divisions – none of this comes from malice. It comes from love. Ridiculous.

Having said that Calpol is too mild to help the delinquent parent anyway, Medised is a different story. It sends them right to sleep, and there are no real medical grounds for sending them to sleep, except that you really wish they would go to sleep. I definitely have used it for exactly that purpose, when T was just under one and we were at a wedding, only I had been called away from the festivities to put him to bed. He was teething, at least. He wasn't entirely, 100% healthy. So I'm still in the top, what, 50% of parents. I would still get a D in GCSE parenting. Medised has a sting in its tail, though, which is that it occasionally goes the opposite way – instead of going to sleep, they go hyperactive. This, serendipitously, corresponds to the other way we deal with our inadequacies – when I don't quite have the stomach to claim that I'm brilliant, compared with those shysters I just fabricated, I might fall back on, "Yes, I did that bad thing, but I was immediately paid back for it with a hyperactive child." Even if my morals are bit flaky, the outcome of this narrative was a good one: my child is protected from my deficiencies by the laws of an ethical universe. That's why people go on and on about sugar, even though sugar has no impact on children at all, apart from making them want more of it, as it does to all of us.

I just met a woman on the common who had Medisedded her daughter at the beginning of a flight to Cape Town and she'd nutted out the whole way there.

Or did I?

There was a phase when T was about 10 months old, during which he would reach a new milestone just about every day. So whenever C came in from work, I'd go, "Guess who climbed six stairs today? No, guess, guess!" and without fail, C would say: "Supervised?" "Well, yes of course he was supervised," I might say, or, "No, I was actually in the cinema at the time, but he must have climbed them 'cause when I got back he was checking his emails," or, "Why do you even leave him with me, if you think you have to ask a question like that?" depending on whether my dial was on Regular, Sarcastic or Angry, but at heart I was always aggrieved, because at heart I was totally convinced there was no safer place T could be than on my watch.

The total opposite is the case. Falling in love with a baby improves your skill set in no respect, except that you now know how to be in love with a baby. I was no better at risk analysis, my spatial awareness had not improved, my decision-making while asleep or half-asleep still sucked.

So, T first fell out of bed when he was three weeks old. The memory of this feels like classic post-traumatic stress. I can see it as if I were floating above it – that dreadful thud, the awful cry where it dawns on all of you what's just happened. C is actually very good with calamity: he never asks that "What was he doing at the edge of the bed in the first place?" question that I, conversely, can't resist and like to spice up with swearwords. Tiny babies are just impossible to work out, in injury terms. They get over things almost immediately, but they are so small that you can't work out whether they've stopped crying because they feel better, or because they've run out of steam. They sleep half the day, so you don't know whether it's a snooze or a concussion. Well, clearly, their not being able to talk doesn't help. It's just hideous. I remember sitting all day, with the curtains drawn, staring at him, wondering whether to take him to casualty. There's only one answer to this, which is don't let them fall out of bed. It wasn't till I had my daughter that I realised what this actually entails – every time you put them on a bed, you have to wonder whether or not they could fall off it.

I'm doing that worse-parent thing again, but this one is definitely true – a friend of a friend put her baby on a washing machine (no, I don't know why, I'm afraid: this is a real person, not one whose motivations I can just make up), while she answered the phone, and the baby naturally fell off the washing machine. The friend on the phone, who was, by good fortune, a paediatrician, said mildly, "Well, maybe just nip into A&E to check" and revealed, months later, that she could tell from the pitch of the baby's cry that it had fractured its skull. So I never did anything as bad as that.

We did, however – and when I fall back on "we", that is a marker of how I don't actually have room in my psyche to take on full responsibility for this – leave the staircase open, and T fell off it, and he broke his collarbone. Well, sure, it's only a collarbone. They heal beautifully in children, apparently. The paediatrician talked of the healing in such glowing terms, he made it sound as though if you didn't break your collarbone in childhood you were missing a wonderful opportunity. Our household stupidity was no longer amusing, from this point, and apart from banisters ("Are you going to get your builder to do you a stable door, while he's there?" said my puckish friend), we now have all kinds of safety features in our house, not least that we are on such a perpetual state of red alert that we haven't in six months used the phrase, "Oh, he/she'll be all right." And I have to say, H has had many fewer accidents than T. Probably the worst thing that's happened to her is that she touched a hot frankfurter when she wasn't expecting it.

C claims that this is because she isn't as intrepid as T was.

That idiot.

CHAPTER 8
Never the same again

*Does motherhood make you
kinder or just more stupid?*

If you think of it like an episode from Without a Trace, all the things people mention about pregnancy – the food, the indigestion, the not being able to remember your pin number even though it's been the same since you were 15 – these are all like the hats and scarves and text messages of the missing person. They are peripheral; from the very get-go, you have lost your va-va-voom, you are not yourself. There you are, going about your business, still in your jeans and state of ignorance, and nevertheless something is awry between you and the world. Even before you hit the displeasing paradox of pregnancy, where the bigger you are, the more invisible you become, it just isn't the same. I have thought about it a lot, because I was in a filthy mood the whole way through both pregnancies, even when I didn't know I was pregnant. My main craving, apart from for haddock, was for an enormous argument every day. In between the end of one conflict and the confection of another, I did stop to wonder what on earth was going on. Is that really what was bothering me: not getting enough attention? Or getting attention for the wrong thing (being pregnant – man alive, you have to have a lot of conversations about being pregnant, when you are pregnant)? No, I think in the end it's all as simple and yet as devilish as low blood sugar and tiredness. I had a diabetic friend at university who shouted at me while we were waiting by a kebab van more times than – well, no, as many times as – I've actually had a kebab.

So, anyway, it happens, and your whole mind is blown, and you think then: I am a totally different person. You wouldn't even stop to count the ways: there is nothing about your old self left – it has been entirely obliterated by love. That sounds like a nice thing, doesn't it? In fact, it is like someone has unleashed some white phosphorus on your personality. There's nothing left, just gnarly lumps.

Unfortunately, I can't really remember the specifics of all this. That's what the non-parent, specifically the pregnant non-parent, always wants: they want you to leave out the "mind-blowing" this and the "changed for ever" that and actually give a specific example. Have you gone off your friends? Have you lost interest in current affairs? Have you gone from a sweet tooth to a salty tooth, have you stopped or started boozing, do you get on better or worse with your mother, are you more or less interested in soap operas? Can't remember, I'm afraid.

Have you got more or less energy? Are you more or less vain, are you more or less trivial, can you concentrate better or less well? Nope, it's all gone. I remember being intensely euphoric, and very emotional. I remember listening to a midwife on the radio; she was from Holland (you have to imagine this said in quite a gruff but kindly Netherlands accent) and she said, "When a baby is born, a mother is born also." And I thought that was the sweetest, most moving thing I'd ever heard. I think I literally had to stand still and gather myself for a minute. But then, probably the very same day, the health visitor came round and gave me a leaflet about testicular cancer, told me to check T and then pointed at C and said, "You need to check his as well." And I cried for about an hour. I wasn't feeling at my very most alluring anyway, and suddenly I was going to have to start chasing the males round the house, feeling their nads, like a veterinary nurse.

This is what used to make me so sceptical about the whole thing. Parents would say their entire lives had been turned upside down, but you could never see this seismic change in attitudes reflected in their behaviour – they didn't appear to be any less daft than they were before. They would say you couldn't comprehend such unimaginable love, but for the 99% of the time that they weren't saying that, they were moaning about how early they'd got up, and fantasising about their children going to sleep. They would say they were happier than they'd ever been in their lives, but they seemed to complain a lot more. It was all quite contradictory.

Doing it didn't make it any more comprehensible. It just made the contradictions seem more inevitable, more obvious.

I definitely am happier, and I definitely complain more, am harder to live with, control my emotions less well, get annoyed more easily. I think this is as simple as sleep deprivation. When T and H get to adolescence, and they want to sleep all day, and I'm the one herding the household out of bed, I bet you I'll be the same as I was five years ago. Though I'll likely be menopausal, so that'll put a new spin on things. I remember when T was about eight months, saying hangovers *were* worse with children, but at the same time I didn't know how anybody coped without children… because they were so sweet, it cheered you up just looking at them. Yeah, that was just hormones talking. Hangovers are brutal with children. When I properly grow up, which now means when *they* grow up, I'm going to take package holidays where children aren't allowed. Maybe I'll move into a gated community where children aren't allowed, just so I can drink myself totally stupid.

I wouldn't say that I take things more or less seriously – I'm definitely not a more serious person – but (this annoys non-parents and I can see why) I feel things more deeply. I'm not saying I feel things more deeply than *you*. I was just a very facile, weak-minded person before, and I now feel things more deeply than that. However, the environment terrors, where I couldn't believe I'd created new life at the very tail end of a livable planet; where I was thinking of hoarding rice, and teaching T how to make fire with sticks, and maybe prior to that, learning myself how to make fire with sticks; where I was going to rig up a bike that could transport a child and a dog, in case we had to get out of the city in an environmental emergency; where I was wondering whether to arrange a kind of house-share with someone who lived on high ground, so they could part-live with us while London still existed, and we could, erm, entirely live with them once it didn't; where I would go to bed muttering "sex, fellowship and the life of the mind", on days when I was so sure the market economy was on the way out that I didn't know what T would have left to enjoy, once he was an adult... all that stuff was just hormones. Perhaps I was right – it's definitely possible. But I definitely don't think like that now.

There is an awful rawness, where you can picture catastrophe befalling your child so vividly that it's almost a
hallucination. But that doesn't last either. That probably
could have lasted a bit longer, in my case, and then maybe
I would have fixed it so that T didn't fall off the stairs.

I was certainly, immediately, more affected by news
stories – cruelty to children, armed conflict of any kind, but
particularly situations with a lot of civilian casualties. It just
means children, doesn't it, "civilian"? That's what we're
really upset about. We're not thinking, "That adult wasn't
a soldier! He/she did not sign up to be killed!" I used to
think people were just being silly to put a premium on a
child's life, that it was part of a stupid death etiquette, the
way you're supposed to care more when a British person
gets killed than an Austrian.

My best friend, J, said when her oldest daughter was
about one, the only thing that's really changed is that your
happiness is now entirely contingent upon theirs. In the
pantheon of Things Parents Say, I thought that was incredibly milky and not very revealing. It sounded a bit like a
holiday-home contract: your deposit repayment is contingent upon the condition of the property when you leave.
That's it on its nose, though – everything else dies down,
the madness subsides, the brain kind of reballs itself from its
marshmallow, you slowly rein in the graphic selfishness of

the beginning bit (it's not even selfishness, it's more atavistic than that: every waking moment is a Titanic-lifeboat
struggle, your baby against every conceivable threat. You
would happily elbow a passerby to death in this condition,
though luckily your reactions aren't fast enough, and
besides, people very rarely try to harm babies. I've certainly
never seen it).

What you're left with is a person upon whom all your
happiness depends, so the whole experience has ruined
your life and in the same stroke made it. But otherwise, all
that fuss over your identity? You're exactly the same as you
were before.

There are two phenomena: one is the memory loss and all-
round fog of pregnancy, and this is known as "preghead",
and the other is the same for when your baby's tiny, and
this is known as "nappy brain". Distinct from all that is
"mumming down", where you emerge from the whole
thing permanently much stupider than you were before.
This is more depressing. But there is good news about the
memory, although unfortunately I don't believe it.

Researchers in Australia did a long-term study that
showed no loss of memory during pregnancy, after all. Why,
in that case, do mothers all adopt the habit of saying out

loud what they're leaving the room for, every time they leave the room? Look at your own mother, who still does this. When she walks out, she goes, "I'm going for a wee." Does your dad do that? Of course not. It's an aide-memoire, a throwback to the days after your birth when she would otherwise have forgotten what she went for, made a cup of tea instead and then wet herself on the way back.

I've still not recovered my memory: I still have to recite a list of things I'm about to do, then count them, then recite them again, if I am to have any hope of remembering even half of them. H's first sentence is going to be, "Gotta find my charger." Seriously, if you were to track my brain activity, it would just dart randomly about within a small, fixed perimeter, like one of those rats that's been given ecstasy.

The most accurate way to measure how much your memory has been screwed by actual pregnancy (rather than life, or alcohol) is to read a book about pregnancy and see how much you can remember of it once you have a one-year-old child. Choose this one, if you like. I can only remember two things from all the parenting books I've ever read: there's an early Doctor Spock that says, "Try to relax while breastfeeding, perhaps with a beer or a cigarette." And there's a bit in the Rough Guide to Pregnancy where her thighs get so chubby that when she walks down the street wearing cords, it sounds like she's having a sword fight.

That's it. I've retained more about how to home-bake your own dog treats than I have about how to bring up children.

As for proper, lasting stupidity, it's hard to tell. I don't have any control data, but I have noticed that my appetite for incredibly thick books has skyrocketed, so, you know, that's probably a bad sign. I asked my sister whether she'd read any really thick books since D was born, and she said "I've read We Need to Talk About Kevin and Infinite Jest," and I said, "Those aren't thick", and she said, "Infinite Jest is *really* thick", and then I had to explain that no, I meant dumb, and she looked at me quite witheringly and said, "I wouldn't waste my time."

Ha! I love to waste my time. It's not just *my* time I waste, either. I wasted the first night out that me and C had together after T was born, dragging him to a rubbish film of the rubbish book I was reading. Anyone would think we were *made* of time. From the minute I got pregnant, for about a year, I read nothing but bodice-rippers. I ran through about four centuries, historical undergarment by historical undergarment. It was horribly compelling, all the self-hate of a sex addiction with no actual sex, and that nauseous, bulimic cognition that however much there was of this book, it was never going to be enough. On the very rare nights when I could put Elizabeth and her bogus virginity aside for one hour to talk to an actual person, a friend, in the world, I would have this burning sense that I had something to recommend, and I'd start a sentence like, "I'm reading the most fantastic book…" Then I'd realise how that sentence would have to end (with an embossed cover… with breasts on the front… by Philippa Gregory). It was like going, "I've found the most marvellous little restaurant. It's called McDonald's".

I read an interview with Tracy Chevalier, in which she said she'd written Girl with a Pearl Earring while she was pregnant, and while other people find themselves impaired by pregnancy, she found that her mind had never been sharper. I can't evaluate that at all, though, having never read her book. Even though it's historical and it looks like there is probably sex in it, it's still way beyond me.

After I'd got through all the sex that might, with some imagination, have happened between all the nobles in the early-modern period, I spent a year reading nothing but newspapers. The longest thing I would ever read would be an article in a heavyweight magazine. I picked up a load of impressionistic word portraits of, say, the pirate scene in Somalia (which is pretty heavy, man), or what a toy factory might look like in China. It wasn't the kind of information that would transport you, and nor could I usefully rip it off. It just existed in my head for a short time, before my nappy brain erased it.

And now I have not so much graduated as lurched into crime, but since I have a new squeamishness, I have to look away from the page if I suspect anything bad is going to happen, so I've reached the end of whole trilogies, whole oeuvres, never entirely sure who is and who isn't dead.

Is this what they mean by mumming down? Can you think of anything else they might mean?

My stepmother is very into the accretion of beliefs, across whole societies, that directly contradict the evidence in front of people's noses, and one of her favourite examples is misogyny. How can people ever have thought that women were stupider than men, when girls are so much faster to talk than boys? Well, at the risk of shoring up sexism – well no, there is no risk of that: we're in a post-contraceptive age and this is a thought about the past (the actual past, not the past as an elaborate backdrop for saucy, made-up gossip) – at a time when any adult pre-menopausal woman would have been either pregnant, having a miscarriage or breastfeeding *all* the time, you'd have to wonder about them a bit. I'm not saying it was ever OK to deny us the protection of the rule of law or reduce us to top-end chattel in the incipient marketplace. But you would have to wonder.

*

Anna Friel's motto is, "Work like you're not being paid, love like you've never been hurt and dance like there's no one watching." It's very naff, and very trite, and for God's sake she's an actress, so even if she were quoting the Dalai Lama it would ill behove you to try to live by her glib motto. Who lives by a motto anyway?

She's right, though, isn't she? I mean, if you could do all those things the way she says you should do them, it would be pretty good.

Vincent Gallo says, "I think the greatest thing you can do as a human being is to be a good parent. That's the most radical impact you can have with your life. The children of good parents, they spread productivity for years to come. And the most evil thing that you can contribute to mankind is destructive parenting." You know, all the same reservations apply, only more so because Gallo seems pretentious where Friel does not, and he is also the man who loved George Bush because he averred that you could gauge the worth of a president by looking at how much the French hated him (it's not without wit, the sentiment. But it's a little bit frickin' stupid). Nevertheless, there it is. The pretentious actor is onto something: you cannot contribute more, unless you are going to create something extraordinary and lasting *as well*, and I'm definitely not going to do that (too tired). It would be perfect to look back on a life and know that you'd done parenting superbly (what's the verb? Parented? Sounds horrible, like you helped a cow give birth). This is not the same, might even be the ideological opposite of a "charity begins at home" credo: you want to be a good parent because you love nothing more than your child, yes. But if you could just get this right, if you could find a way to lavish all your unarguable love that wasn't cloying or spoiling, that didn't annoy or stunt them, that made them fearless not arrogant, that made them generous not lordly, that made their possibilities seem infinite, then would that not help to create a *cool person* for the rest of the world to enjoy? Come on.

So this is what we all think: we would absolutely love to be a great parent. How do you go about this, exactly? First, according to the books, while you're planning the pregnancy you and your partner have to discuss your worldviews and make sure they're not unbridgeably different. They always, *always* use the example, "Is it OK with both of you if your children grow up to be gay?" You know what they're thinking: "What counts as a controversy these days? Erm, racism, sexism, anti-semitism... but we can't use any of those – it'll sound like we can imagine normal people, who want to be parents, in a right-thinking world, being racist! And that alone would make *us* racist. Can't use politics. No couples argue about politics, and who would ever have a political argument about a baby? Can't use faith – too incendiary. Let's do the gayers. They're not going to be reading this anyway." Well, maybe it worked for you. For me and C, I would not say this gay conversation was the most revealing one. It did not subtly dust out the potential fissures in our parenting styles. Maybe that's because it was retrospective: by the time we'd seen the inside of any parenting advice, I was already pregnant. Probably the first conversation you're meant to have, before the gay one, is, "Shall we get pregnant?"

In an ante-natal class, the midwife told us to write down the kind of child we wanted to have. This totally baffled me. What kind of child do you want to have? A left-footer? A genius? A rapier wit? One who is really tired at night time? One with a small head? What kind of stupid question is that?

More useful was the exercise where you write down five things you want to repeat about the way your parents were with you, and five things you don't want to repeat. I mulled this over for ages. There was a weekend when I was 16 and worried about my GCSEs, when my mum let me smoke even though she was pretending to think I didn't smoke. I'd like to think I could be as flexible as that. Otherwise, most of my adolescence is lost to the fog of war, and I think the main thing I could extrapolate from that whole period is, "Try to time it so that you're not going through the menopause at the exact same time as your children are going through puberty." Unfortunately, by the day before I got pregnant, it was a bit late for that. The best I could have done would have been to delay it, so that I hit the menopause when they were about 10. And that, as they say, is a risky old game.

I have two pressing memories of coming a very distant second to my mother's job – one when she was meant to come to my primary school and pair me in a maypole extravaganza, and unexpectedly didn't, so that I didn't even have a stand-in adult partner; I had to just carry my whole section on my own. And such is the nature of the maypole, as a dancing form, which could be why it never really caught on, that one person doing it wrong can literally ruin the whole thing for all 35 of you.

Another time... Oh, never mind. It seems petty, and actually I'm coming to the point, which is not that Career Women Make Bad Mothers. Rather, that I think this is revisionism. I think I was embarrassed and disappointed, but I don't think I ever constructed a hierarchy of her priorities and put myself at the bottom, or near the middle. I think that narrative built around it later, mainly because she felt bad about it, or perhaps because I came to understand that she felt bad about it, and recast the incident as ammunition. So from a parenting perspective, the thing I'd try not to repeat wouldn't be unavoidable lateness. Rather, I would try not to refract everything through the prism of my own shortcomings, so that events in the children's lives that they easily had the resilience to handle took on more importance than they needed to, because I banged on about them so much. And yet, having said that, I wouldn't want to just obliterate the fact of my shortcomings – I wouldn't want to erase them from family lore on the off chance that they made memories of events seem worse than the events actually were. It's complicated, isn't it? And it gets 10 times more complicated when the baby is actually there, and you realise that you have no memory at all of how your mother was with you, at that age. All you've got is what she was like when you were eight. When you were a baby, in all likelihood (and this is a behavioural probability), she was exactly as you are with your baby: that's where you learned it. When did the mutual adoration turn into a more, ahem, critical relationship? When did you start to see one another's imperfections?

The idea that you could, in this clear-eyed way, dissect her parenting, separate very simply the good from the bad (what if the good was a consequence of the bad? And vice versa?), and then decide which bits to repeat and which to avoid... I won't say it's nonsensical, but it's quite optimistic. And that's before you've even got to your dad.

Anyway, I asked C what his list would say, what five things he'd like to do, and what five he wouldn't. He said he'd pretty much do it all the same, and I said that was ridiculous. What, everything?

And he said, "You know when you're a kid, and they say, 'Here comes your auntie Angela', but she's not your actual aunt? I'm not going to do that."

CHAPTER 9
Oh no, he's got my personality

Why everyone's child is cleverer than yours

We took T to Centre Parcs with his second cousin, who is also his birth-twin, when they were almost 10 months old. The cliché is that you constantly circle them to see which is the most advanced, but they both seemed broadly to be as idiotic as each other, and besides, there was a more pressing competition. Z (I'm not trying to anonymise him – his name is Zeek) had better stuff. A massive, Ikea-scale stash of plastic, all eerily well suited to withstanding a 10-month-old's delinquent attentions, all fascinating but not toxic or dangerous, all noisy, all flashing, incredibly fun. An incredible explosion of pure fun. It's almost as if there were people whose job it was to design this stuff, just for babies.

I'd pretty much never bought anything for T. I went through a drive of anti-consumerism, following my new-found parental enviro-awareness, though luckily this didn't extend to things I bought for me, only for him. It's pointless buying clothes for boys. From the age of three months, or whenever they're out of the round-the-clock onesie, they dress like little men. Socks, jeans, vest, T-shirt, jumper if it's cold – there you are. A little man. What is the point of spending money on this stuff? In charity shops you can get it practically for free. Girls don't dress like little women; they dress like little girls, so it feels like there's more diversion to be had from dressing them up. Don't get me wrong, though: I didn't spend a fortune on H either. I just did spend some money, maybe £17 per age range, whereas I did not spend any money at all on T, and frankly, until I revisited this policy, he didn't always look his best.

Other people bought him soft toys when he was born, and in a dogless house these would have waited in a cupboard until he was older. But six months is a long time for a dog (technically, it's three and a half years). My brother sent us a puppet elephant, and when I first put my hand in it, Spot went at it with such gusto he nearly took my arm off. I couldn't work out whether he genuinely didn't know I was in there, or whether he'd been wanting to sever my arm for some time and had just been waiting for plausible deniability, as they say in American foreign policy. The elephant, along with two monkeys, unnumbered varieties of rabbit and a very branded Baby Gap bear (my mother lives above a Baby Gap), belonged immediately to the dog.

I'd look at parents' houses and think, why have you got all that tat? Wouldn't you rather just have nice clean surfaces and CDs? I thought I was doing something revolutionary, I thought I was creating a child without material urges, who would look upon the trees and the animal kingdom as his playthings. (We have a dog, remember. What more do you want, a remote control tractor?) All I was creating was a child who was not yet very old. That's how you can tell that there's a real person in there – when they embark upon the frenzied agglomeration of stuff.

Tentatively, then, we came out of our dark idiocy, blinking into the toy department of developed world consumerism. T got a "biscuit jar", where you put biscuits in the hole and there are all these different shapes, and when you get it right, it makes an array of different noises, and... *blah*. That's the other reason I never wanted to get involved with all this: I had this anxiety, which I still have, that you dangle this stuff before them, they thrill with excitement, and then one day they realise that it's just stupid useless stuff, there's no purpose to it. Those aren't even real biscuits, you can't eat them, that music is horrible and it's all just tat. And you gave it to them.

In the best possible scenario, by the time they realise the limitations of one toy, they'll have graduated to incontinent joy at the appearance of something slightly more sophisticated – a walker that spells words, a truck that spews out farm animals, a die-cast metal train. But what if that's not how it works? What if it's all just crushing disappointment, as they realise that gift after gift is just more noisy plastic, that there's nothing behind it?

And while we're here, doesn't the baby get a rubbish deal from the mother-child dyad anyway? We're always complaining about how it's not that demanding, intellectually, chatting to someone who can't chat, but at least the babies are changing all the time. Mothers alter very little. Maybe once in a blue moon we have new hair.

The first six weeks, probably six months, really lull you into a false sense of security, as you fill the time with gazing, seeing other adults, inviting them to gaze. Then suddenly, or maybe little by little if you were paying attention, they become demonstrably conscious. Suddenly, it strikes you that sitting there making a funny face is no longer enough. Your timetable, where you spend an hour getting out of the house and then just walk around – this might not be enough either. This is probably incredibly boring. A cardboard box, a stick that isn't sharp, a crisp packet – none of these things are that interesting any more. With your firstborn, you have absolutely nothing in place, you have nothing in your psychic toolbox for keeping someone company who now needs company.

C was immediately brilliant at it, because he is fundamentally foolish. He had all these elaborate games, like, imagine the travel changing mat is in fact a surfboard, and the rug is instead the sea, and C himself is an innocent surfer, just surfing along the rug – sorry, sea – except that one of his arms is a shark, and then it starts to attack his leg, and Oh! Oh! Will his leg escape from his arm?

This was hilarious to T.

Tsk, I used to think, as he roared away and C surfed past. I don't know where all this fun comes from. Who wakes up in the morning and thinks, "Today I'm going to surf across the floor, repackaging my body parts as different sea creatures"? And how does a person who has never seen a shark, and only rarely seen the sea, and never seen a surfer, find this funny? And where is *my* sense of infinite ludic possibility?

My sister used to put her baby and mine in a cot, and then get underneath it and bark, and they'd think this was the funniest thing ever, even though there was no real "underneath" to the cot, and they could clearly see her lying on the floor.

I had nothing in my comic armoury, nothing unless you count throwing a tea towel over my head and then leaping out. It was pathetic. Sometimes I would tramp across the common, on the phone to my sister, complaining about how uninteresting it must be for T to just watch me tramping across the common, on the phone to her. She said maybe I was depressed.

Someone else said I should get off my arse and go to a playgroup.

That was when one of those terrible parent transitions happened to me. I took T and D to some organised play event, where there's a format, and other babies, and mothers, and two young women at the front with a Plan, which involves yelling in a partially musical, systematised way, sometimes with instruments. D absolutely hated it. She hated it this time, and every subsequent time, and when she was old enough to walk in, she would walk straight out again, and even by the time she had mustered so much lupine cunning that she'd found the biscuits meant for the mums and stolen them before I even realised she'd stopped screaming, she hated it.

But this was the first time I realised how much she hated it and, you know, I didn't know how to read her displeasure. It might not have been the event she hated – perhaps someone had spilt boiling lava on her. I couldn't tell what T made of it, because I couldn't hear him over D, and he was in the pushchair facing forwards. He could have been smoking crack or doing a Rubik's cube. Anyway, "I don't care," I thought. "We've come all the way here now, and we are definitely going to enjoy ourselves."

Even before I'd arranged that thought into words, I had a The Parent Speaks moment. You know when you're a kid, and your parent says a thing like that, you think, "Well, why? Why do we have to force some fun out of the day? Why can't we just surrender ourselves to the fact that sometimes you arrive somewhere and it doesn't look like that much fun after all?" And you take this flexibility all the way into adulthood, and maybe you schlep all the way across town to a poetry reading that turns out to be quite literally a load of people reading poetry... What the hell? You can just leave.

Then suddenly, wham. One minute ago, you thought parenthood had brought only good things to the table of your personality, but not so. Next I'll be inching my way round art galleries like my legs are tied together, scowling at people who move at a reasonable pace.

None of these problems ever arises twice, because once you have a second child, and it turns into a person, the first is already right there, demanding interesting events every second of its waking day anyway. There is no way you could be too boring for a second child, and even if you were, the first child would entertain it for you. But I am still keenly aware of my uselessness in this area. It wasn't depression

– I really was useless. Playgroup eventually sort of worked, but only up to a point. As soon as there was another mother I could talk to, I would desert my sandcastle or pan pipes or half-arsed pretence at a sea war between plastic lizards, and blather on instead. There is no conversation on earth so boring – not my own health, my dog's health, the weather – that I don't find it more interesting than getting on my hands and knees and concocting amusement from objects. All that anxiety over toys was really just the displaced fear that if either child – any child – scrutinised me too closely, they would realise how fundamentally tedious I was, how there was nothing behind me, how I was all plastic and noise. Once I put it like that, I feel far better about it. I can't play cricket, either. I can't play a mouth organ or speak any languages apart from on menus. What am I going to do, shoot myself?

My mother came round one day when T was maybe seven months old, with a waterproof bathtime book for him, only he was too busy thumping the floor to take any notice, so she showed it to me. "Look, it's inflatable."

"Yes, that's brilliant. He'll love that."

"It says, 'Hey, hey, what do you say, it's time to take our bath today!'"

"Yeah, that's great."

"Bring your duckie! Bring your boat! Bring your toys that like to float!"

Hang on a tick...

"Gently scrub from top to toes..."

She's reading me the book! This can't be happening. She'll be giving me a bath next – there won't be anything I can do about it.

"Now I kiss you on the nose."

"You're reading me the book!"

"I am not," she says stoutly. "I'm just telling you what it says."

This, by the way, is one value I imbibed so wholesale from my mother that I didn't even stop to think about it until just now: she would always buy us books. It didn't matter if she was skint, or in a bad mood, or we were in the doghouse, or grounded, or on bail, or whatever – we were always allowed books, whatever books we wanted. It was as if they existed in a separate, parallel economy, where money still exists but all the rules are different. Like with truffles, and art. I say I never bought T anything, but I spent a fortune on books for him to chew, when he could have chewed pretty much anything.

My friend told me that they start looking at books when they're three months old, because he distinctly remembered reading his son Where the Wild Things Are at Christmas.

So, from when T was about two months old, I bought him crinkling books and rattling books, and books of animals and books where you can literally stick your finger into the protagonist and make him waggle about (who knew such things existed?). I bought him books of babies, and black-and-white books of baby animals, and reflective books where a baby who is concentrating can see his face and fancy the book to be all about him.

Someone bought him a book that made a tractor noise. I look back now and give a bitter laugh for the time when that solitary book, that ambient, soothing tractor sound, was the most annoying noise in the house.

My mum bought him the bath book.

Someone else bought him a Gruffalo compendium, and I declared the stories unreadable, but they're only unreadable when you have a child who isn't listening.

I bought him new books and secondhand books that he was allowed to rip up if he felt like it. I bought him pop-up books, even though I think they were invented to create built-in obsolescence for children's books – they have to break, otherwise they last for ever. How do you break a book? Why, you add all these additional breakable flaps. There's one about a mole with a turd on his head that lasted so short a time I think it was actually the business model for the iPod. I got out library books and I nicked books off my sister.

T continued to ignore them all. By six months, he had got to the stage of sticking them in his mouth. If you tried to open them and show him anything, he would look at you with gentle patience, as if to say, "No, no, no, dear, you can stick these things in your mouth, you know."

I bought him every possible variant of those beautifully drawn books where dinosaurs do naughty things. I obsessed over his lack of interest, and I made an ill-advised remark about how we should be role-modelling reading for pleasure (ill-advised because now, still, whenever C is loafing about reading the paper and I make to hassle him about loafing about, he goes, "Darling, I'm role-modelling reading for pleasure.")

My friend P's daughter still couldn't talk at all by the time she was two. Some people thought they'd heard her say "off", but they couldn't be sure. She got a private speech therapist in, who wrote an incredibly long report, the short version of which was, "Pushy mother."

I thought, maybe that's it, I'm conveying some kind of performance anxiety. I've thrown him off the scent that this might be an enjoyable item, by staring at him with my brow furrowed every time he goes near it. My words say, "Look at this exciting book!" My face says, "It carries disease." This is before you consider the fact that the only way he could viably be kept still was if I wrestled him to my side, clamped him there with one arm and turned the pages with the other. He never made any fuss about this, but I did once notice that by the end of We're Going on a Bear Hunt I was actually sweating and he still wasn't listening.

But imagine how much *fun* that was.

Yeah, what that Where the Wild Things Are friend actually meant was "a year and three months". The mistake I made, as a neurotic first-time mother, was to believe things that people told me. Another friend told me that her daughter had eaten the end off a French loaf, just nuzzled away at it surreptitiously from inside her papoose, when she was six weeks old. What she actually meant was six months. My advice is that if anyone says anything, from their own memory of parenthood, that makes you think your baby is retarded, add a year to whatever it is they said, and reconsider.

They never have anything to say in baby development books about crawling. According to the (frankly nutty) author of the What to Expect... series, this is because it's not an index of anything: some babies just never do it. Still, it's a big deal: it's definitely the one you tick off in the My Baby books. They never have a line in those saying, "Baby's first fine motor movement."

In the 1950s (I got a vintage baby book off eBay, instead of a proper new one, because I am stupid), the terminology was still up for grabs, and you could use "creep" and "crawl" interchangeably, like with insects. There's a section for you to fill in, that goes "Baby first creeps:" into which I could have written "eight months and four days", if C hadn't already written, "I think my mummy's really pretty" in the space. Like that's funny.

Anyway, some observations about creeping. It doesn't arrive fully fledged, like a gift from the skies. Before you ascend to the ranks of excellent crawling, you have to go through the stage of being a rubbish crawler. There he'd go, poor little fellow, heaving himself across the floor like a fattie on an army exercise, while me and C sat on the sofa going, "It looks like hard work, doesn't it?" "Yeah... Isn't it nice once you've learned how to do it, and you can just sit around?" Also, crawling doesn't arrive on its own – it's really just one of a range of skills in the portfolio "Can seek danger". Waiting till you've been put somewhere high by someone who isn't concentrating, and then wriggling; hurling, pitching, flinging yourself; being fearless; grabbing things that are hot/sharp/alive/toxic. All this stuff arrives at exactly the same time. As a mother, it's as if you've spent eight months looking after a cushion, and suddenly you're in charge of a self-harming conger eel.

What I found strange, just from a survival-of-the-species point of view, is that you'd think the accretion of skills would occur in tandem, so a small new physical capability would be accompanied by a small amount of sense, and you would criss-cross, developmentally, between the physical and the mental, like Spiderman going up a wall. What happens in real life is that a huge raft of new physical prowess just arrives, accompanied by no sense whatsoever. One day T didn't know the bed had an edge. The next day he couldn't rest until he'd chucked himself off it.

D had a different crawling technique, or maybe it was the same technique, but the difference was that you'd never see her do it. I don't mean, "You never see her do it, even though you see her every fortnight." I mean, I saw her all the time, and I never saw her crawl. I was just aware that she'd moved because she was never where I'd left her. My sister said she was like the London Eye – you couldn't see her movement because it was perpetual. That was the first time it occurred to me that T and D might have two distinct personalities, rather than being just male/female variants of Baby.

So that's the order: first you acquire the physical skills you need to injure yourself; at around the same time, you get a personality; and at some point in the future, you get some sense. What kind of a cock-eyed way round is that? How did we all even survive into adulthood?

I thought that was all there was to it, once he could crawl. I totally forgot that crawling is just a staging post on the way to walking. It's like watching your grandmother go over sheet ice, only you can't help because you haven't got your shoes on. It's also incredibly destructive and much faster than it looks. Yeah, if I'm honest, it totally ruined my holiday. All my holidays, for a whole year.

Following a fraught week in the Lake District (when I say "fraught", I mean "shit": "fraught" is actually a universally accepted term to make "shit" sound more mature)... Sorry, we had this fraught week; let me précis it for you. T could not be transported up any mountains – he was too heavy and his buggy was too rubbish – so we thrashed out an imperfect system, where C went with all the fun childless people up the mountain, like, 12 times (he would say "twice"), and stayed behind looking after T once while I went, only I didn't have any reception up a mountain, so I couldn't constantly call and check everything was OK. I can't remember anything at all about the walk – all I remember is about 5% of the million fatal childcare errors I dreamed up. It would have been more fun and less stressful for me to put one of those aerobics steps in front of the telly and just get on and off it.

Anyway, after that I decided to pare the holiday experience right back – still go away but not spend any money. We went to my stepmother's house, by the beach, and by this time T was nearly walking. It was carnage. There hasn't been such wanton destruction of tiny decanters and small hand mirrors since Cromwellian times. I kept looking at him, beaming away with a knick-knack in his hand, and I'd be thinking, "I've got time to put down this coffee before he breaks... *Nooo!*"

So that cost me a lot in goodwill. I decided that money was actually cheaper, and next we went to a villa in Italy. Here he walked in earnest, holding out his arms like a tightrope walker with inexplicably fat arms. I came to understand what parents mean when they say they're proud of their children – before it seemed a little far-fetched to claim their achievements, or even their attributes, as your own. I mean, where's that going to end, if you're going to congratulate yourself for a good genetic legacy? Are you going to launch into a song of praise every time you look in a mirror, or get a fork into your mouth?

Happily, I can now shine a light on this feeling. It's not rational pride, forged out of a thought process along the lines of, "I did thing X. It is good. I did a good job." (I realise I'm starting to adopt the syntax of Thomas the Tank Engine.) It is a totally irrational wellspring of emotion that just leaps out of your heart when they achieve the smallest, most quotidian task. It's one of those things you can set against all the other things you're continually moaning about. A bad idea to interrogate it too closely – you don't want your heart to realise it's ridiculous and stop leaping.

Walking is incredibly endearing to watch, at every level. When they suck at it, it is funny to see them waddling along. When they get pretty good at it, it is amazing. Even though you know this is what humanity looks like – you rarely see a four-year-old who hasn't learned to walk – you still think something bizarre has happened, like the dog's got up on its hind legs and started wearing an apron. Perhaps I was anthropomorphising, but when we got back from Italy with T walking, I swear the dog kept looking at him like, "Pal, I thought we were on the floor together? I thought it was you and me against those bipeds?"

Food is exactly the same as toys, although of course we have our own baggage to contend with here. Few adults (I'd think) have a massive emotional carousel of toy-attitudes; nutrition is a bit more elemental. You're meant to have a primal urge to get food into them, and I think this is true up to a point, although, like other primal urges, it is possible to contain it for periods of time. It's also got more social connotations (broadly, common people feed their kids crisps; the main swathe of the middle class favours straightforward, underseasoned sausage-and-broccoli combinations but doesn't disallow sugar; there's a branch of the urban middle class that is insane and seeks to power its offspring on quinoa, with perhaps a raisin sweetened with grape concentrate on a birthday; and the posh don't care. That's it, broadly. I don't know why I'm telling you this, like you're some kind of space visitor. Obviously you have a class of your own, and you'll know perfectly well what goes on in it).

I should be in the quinoa class, but in fact I don't care. I'm obviously very aspirational – I'm trying to squeeze into the aristocracy via my children's lower intestines. But of course when T was a baby, I cared like a tigress. It never extended to the creed of organic goods (I sometimes accidentally buy them; I sometimes accidentally like people who believe in them; but I would never in a million years join those neurotic ranks of witch-hunt-level superstition, where people intone darkly, "Have you noticed how much autism there is now, when we're constantly eating pesticides? Do you know how many antibiotics you get off an inorganic cowburger?").

T started, as all babies start, on puree. I heard a You and Yours once, years before I had children, where someone whose expertise I have totally forgotten said not to mix tastes, because they wouldn't be able to pick out what they liked from what they didn't like. You should introduce them to foods as a pure experience first; when you are confident that you know their basic predilections, you can experiment. I'm not some Radio 4 automaton that just does everything it says – I don't have an Isa or anti-badger net. But I did do this, slavishly, baking beetroot on a separate shelf from carrot, poaching this, braising that (I know these words mean the same thing; I'm trying to create the chimera of variety), and he would just open up his mouth and spirit it away. (Somebody said, "It's very male, that – girls always want to get hold of the spoon." I thought she was calling him slow and wrote off her opinions as wrong from every conceivable angle, but having since had a girl, that is 100% true.) I'd watch people with fussy toddlers, my sister basically, and say, "Oh well, T will eat anything", literally say that out loud, as if the happy combination of my superior child and my superior parenting self-evidently resulted in more nutritious meals and better household health.

Yeah. The forbearance it took not to say anything to me, to just smile mildly and wait for me to discover for myself what toddlers will and won't eat, is dwarfing. I would have had to pinch or slap me.

I was very rigid on the following things: I was never uptight about food order, and I always insisted on a pudding, whether that was before or after the main course. I didn't want to set up a dialectic (if you like) between sweet and savoury, I wanted them to be morally interchangeable. I was convinced (this was at the start, you understand, not now that I have some sense) that the only reason kids go crazy for sweets is that they have a constitutional understanding that sweets are forbidden, and forbidden things are better. If chocolate were as much of a duty as peas, then it would never have any cachet. What I have discovered is what the rest of the world already knew and has always known: the forbidden element is only half the attraction - the other half is that sweets are nicer than almost anything.

So between, say, five and 10 months, you have this adorable child who will eat anything it can pick up. It definitely helps that they're strapped in, but at this stage you don't even realise that: you're not thinking of it as mealtime restraints, you're thinking of it as an ordinary high chair. Incrementally, they go off things, and it never feels like a big deal - so what if he won't eat pureed parsnip? I wouldn't eat pureed parsnip either: this is just part of becoming a man. I took every new rejection with total stoicism. Sure,

I'm a human being – when he declared he didn't like sausages I felt a twang of sadness (I love sausages) – but I never took any of it seriously. Then, wham, you look round and you have a toast-and-yoghurt child. T won't even eat toast reliably. He won't eat yoghurt unless it's a Thomas the Tank Engine yoghurt. He'll eat bacon, olives, peas, Jammie Dodgers. That's it. For every single meal, he is presented with a roughly nutritional split of carbohydrate, protein and vegetation, and he'll patiently sit and pick the protein out of the carbohydrate, but only if it's bacon or olives. He used to eat wonderful stir fries with water chestnuts, and (I never thought this would last) pearl barley risotto, and hearts of palm and baba ganoush and tarka dahl – he used to eat everything. Now he eats like an old man trying to get drunk in a tapas bar. So long as you don't make him use a fork he'll give it a go, but it's basically olives.

CHAPTER 10
And then I did it all again

A second round of careful unplanning

What is the point, really, of a second pregnancy? Well, yes, yes, of course it produces yet another child. If you love the first one, which everybody does, beyond all measure, then most probably you want another just like it. I contend, nevertheless, that your dial is effectively reset by the time your firstborn is one. Before it's one, anything could happen: you could still be insane and think you need 10 children, which, given that you're almost certainly already 34, means you have to get pregnant again now, this instant, no, not after a cup of tea, *now*. Or you could think that breastfeeding once every other day is like taking contraception. Or perhaps you are so in love with your six-month-old that the bittersweet yearning of watching it grow makes you want another. All those things can happen. That's why "Irish twins" exist (these are siblings born in

the same 12 months. Not actual twins, born in Ireland –
those don't have quote marks).

If you can navigate all that without repregnantising
yourself, you're back where you started, before you even
had one: viz you know you want another, and you know
theoretically that you'll love it. But otherwise, all you can
see is the sprawling inconvenience, and it furthermore seems
improbable that you'll love it as much as you love the first
one. You're really just thinking of it as a large, animated toy
for the first one: a toy, on the one hand; relief, on the other,
from the relentless company of just you, its parents; and on
the third hand, a personality corrective because it is already
a little bit spoilt. It's not quite as iffy as having a second child
to harvest its kidney, but it's in that ballpark.

There's something about the conception of the second
child, then, that fosters a particular kind of conversation.
Among parents of only one child, it's a rueful "Do you think
you'll have another?", half hoping for nice news (it is always
nice news, isn't it?), yet half hoping for a partner in crime
who says, "I don't know if I can be bothered. Can you
be bothered?" Non-parents say, "Are you going to have
another?" because, to their mind, your answer will give a
genuine reading on how happy you are to have one. They
don't understand that you might totally adore that one from
every angle, and yet still want not want to duplicate it, let

alone have another one that isn't even the same. They have reason on their side, you must concede. But you have... you have the nobbly, incomprehensible texture of lived human experience. Some people just don't want another.

Parents of two or more children say, "When are you going to have another?" in a jolly, hectoring, "Come on, look lively, do your bit" tone, a side-order of smugness since they've already done it (I'm talking about me again: this is the tone I like to adopt) and the very faintest whiff of outrageous intrusiveness (How's your sex life? How are those ovaries coming along? Is his sperm swimming in the right direction? Does he eat enough broccoli? What's your pin?).

This is acceptable – fine, even – because people expect to be patronised by someone who's got one child more than them. The exception is if you've had one and you're talking to a twin-pregger: you're not allowed to patronise her because she's probably been breathless and ready to fall over since about week 12. There is nothing you can tell her about labour, either, since you've only ever done it one at a time. It would be like trying to tell a footballer's girlfriend about sex. And actually, even if you have had five, and you meet a twin-pregger with one already, you still can't patronise her. All you can really do with someone carrying twins is make a nice, sympathetic face (though my mum likes to digest the news, and then go "Fuck! What are you going to do?", like there's a whole raft of options, such as having them in instalments or freezing yourself until they're older). While we're talking about twins, once they're born you're not allowed to say "IVF?" even though, for some reason I can't put my finger on, when you see two babies of roughly the same age who aren't identical, that is all you want to know.

Having said that, my very good friend with twins who are a bit older than T says that not only did people constantly ask her whether they were IVF, they asked her questions on a level of nosiness that I couldn't even dream about, questions about her hormones and his sperm, and did she have chlamydia when she was younger, and were his pants too tight, and had they tried Chinese medicine before they went down the "conventional" route, and one question that I'm too squeamish to type, but I'll give you the clue that it contained the word "viscous".

Anyway, I'm getting there, I'm getting to what happened. The *on dit* is that everybody wants two. My friend J said that you feel you've completed your family when you've replicated what you grew up in. I said, that's bollocks: you've completed it at two, which is, coincidentally, what everybody grew up in, because everybody wants two. She said, "What about the people with three?" and I said, "They are mad."

C says that if we'd actually had a conversation about either pregnancy, he would have started the first one two years after it actually began, and the second one three years after the end of the first one. So in theory, I would be looking to get pregnant in September 2012. But that is not what happened.

Sorry: I am rambling because I don't want to get down to what actually happened. I'm embarrassed.

But this is exactly what happened....

Probably, I had some changes in appetite, but I had been so ferociously appetitive, on and off, since T's very incipience that I'd ceased even to interrogate myself about it. Sometimes I looked OK. Sometimes I looked chubby and couldn't get my clothes on. But over this period, just before Christmas in 2008, I couldn't work up the va-va-voom to care about it. Overwhelmingly, I just felt incredibly tired, and I caught myself making strange decisions based on physical laziness, like, perhaps I could stop reading a newspaper and, that way, could avoid going into the newspaper shop? Possibly the dog didn't need a walk? Would more patting do?

So of course my first thought was cancer.

I also had a new surge of rage against C, which I first noticed when I bought some new boots. He made some wise-ass remark about whether or not I should have discussed it with him before I joined the Gestapo, but then, mistaking my half-hearted laughter for a good mood, he said this genuinely contentious thing: "Is that the best thing to do on days we have childcare? When you can take T with you to go shopping?" I went totally crazy, with the "How *dare* you"s and the "When did you ever take T shopping with *you?*"s, and the rest.

I thought that was parathyroid disease (one of whose symptoms, according to Dr Internet, is: "Spouse claims you are more irritable and harder to get along with (cranky, bitchy).")

I noticed a new, generalised inertia – nothing specific, just a run of bad things happening to me that wouldn't have happened if I'd been paying attention. I went to Mothercare with T and his cousin D, and while I was sifting through the babygros T chewed the end of a swim woggle. You don't need to know what that is, just its dimensions – two metres long, the diameter of a drainpipe, bright red.

"You have to buy it," said someone who was paying more attention than me to any of this. "He's chewed it."

I looked at the end. Imagine you'd gone shopping with a bored goat. That's about what it looked like. I still couldn't believe I had to buy it.

"Well, nobody else is going to buy it."

"They might not notice…" I saw this was a sticky wicket. "Don't you have insurance for this kind of thing?"

"For a baby chewing a swim woggle? No!"

You'll think I was being tight, but I was also very tired, remember. I didn't want to go home with two babies and a swim woggle. Plus, I still wanted to have a fight. Sluggish and furious. Definitely a parathyroid disorder. How could it possibly be anything else?

Of course what I should have done was choose someone who looked like a keen yet incompetent swimmer, and given it away. But I am too frugal.

The next day, I was in the corner shop and I parked T up facing what I thought was coffee, and four or five minutes in, the fella goes, "Your baby has some sugar," and I, thinking I was an old hand at this goat-accompanied shopping, waved airily and said, "I'll buy it" (I did actually need it), and he said, "I don't think that's going to solve this." So I turned round and he'd bitten into it, then held it over his head, so that he was covered – you think "from head to toe" is only an expression, until you see someone covered from head to toe – with a sugar frosting. He looked like a really large and eerily lifelike decorative Christmas elf; his tongue was darting out on explorative facial sugar missions that only made it more eerie. I left the shop (I paid), and got outside to untether the dog, upon which the dog started to lick him as well, and they were tongue-sword-fighting each other for square inches of his face, while I just stood there going, "Oh, stop it! You're both disgusting! Stop it right now!". Finally a taxi driver with a brush in his cab came out and tsked them both down, and then I started crying.

The day after that, we were by the duck pond when T started having this amazing tantrum, which I was totally unprepared for. It would have been OK were it not for the rogue goose element (already enraged by the dog, they basically took T's side against me. That's the only way I could really interpret all the honking and aggressive running). An AA man (they really *are* the fifth emergency service) had to get out of his van to help me wrestle T into his buggy. Later on, I said to C that T had behaved so badly an AA man had to help me, and he said, "Did you *call* the AA?"

Anyway, sluggish, angry, incompetent, tired and probably hungry, I persisted with my parathyroid diagnosis, though of course I never exposed this to the scrutiny of, like, a doctor.

The day after that, I went to the gym and came home thinking nostalgically about a time when I was about 14, and I was in Dorothy Perkins trying to get my dad to buy me a shirt dress in blue jersey, and he said no because I looked like a pregnant duck.

Then the day after *that*, I thought, that's weird. I wonder what made me remember that. Could it be... from the side, is it possible that I look like a duck? A pregnant duck? And I said to C, "Am I mad, or do I look a little bit pregnant?"

He said, "Never mind are you mad; I would have to be mad to answer a question like that. So you are mad just thinking that I'm that mad."

And then I was infuriated.

So the day after *that*, I went to get a pregnancy test, and the day after *that*, I went to the doctor, and the week after *that*, I went to get a private scan because I thought I might, I just might make it in time for the nuchal fold test (13 and a bit weeks). So even though I hate private medicine with all my heart, there I am, because I am spineless and incredibly stupid, in a private clinic for a dating scan. Before you go in, there's a form to fill in on which one of the questions is, "How did you get pregnant?" I was looking for a box marked, "It was dark and I was drunk", but nothing, just a column of expensive-sounding acronyms.

Everybody had a man with them. C was... I can't even remember where C was. I'd done it all in such a rush that I forgot your first scan was meant to be a beautiful moment, where you hold hands. I'd approached this more as an administrative vexation, like when the battery goes on your Honda. The first I knew of it, looking at a grainy black-and-white image that was certainly a baby, I was 20 weeks pregnant. One-half-of-a-pregnancy pregnant. First scans always look tiny and incomprehensible, like coffee beans, which is why every couple's pet name for the foetus (unless it's "Are we absolutely sure about all this?") is Bean, and they all think they're the only ones that do that, but H was enormous. She didn't look like a coffee bean – she looked like a labrador puppy.

Now, the question that comes up at this juncture is, "Haven't women got some kind of lunar system that alerts them to this kind of thing?" And the short answer is, no. Not since T was born have me and the moon been sending one another any kind of messages. The truth is I thought I was having an early menopause (I was 35 and it does happen – I read it in the Daily Mail), and even though I have this craven urge to share almost every conversation I have with the widest possible audience, I don't have the backbone, with a real anxiety, to tell anyone. The simplest conversation, with one friend or acquaintance or – heaven forfend – officer of the medical profession, would have yielded something like, "Oh, I never got my periods back either – that's how I ended up with my second/third/fourth child."

So anyway, I was definitely pregnant. I had missed all the important early pregnancy stuff. I hadn't been taking folic acid, I'd been drinking, I'd smoked (but, as C pointed out helpfully, "only when you were drunk"), I'd missed the test for Down's syndrome and the week before I'd had a meal that started with oysters and reached apotheosis in a ballantine of grey squirrel. And that was just at lunchtime! I can't even remember what I had for tea. There are some foods, probably only about three or four, left in the world that the midwives wouldn't go to the trouble of ruling out, because they cannot imagine any scenario in the developed world where someone would eat one. Squirrel must be one such food, surely?

Naturally I was filled with the miracle of birth and all that, but I was mainly thinking about how incredibly embarrassing this was going to be. It's bad enough having to say you're pregnant in the first place, making this really sudden diversion onto bodily function, in a conversation with someone who, 99 times in 100, you've never even discussed your piercings with (I don't really have any piercings). I have a droll friend who said, "At least you're not young. When young people tell me they're pregnant, all I can think of is that they must have had sex." But this was 10 times worse, because as soon as I said it, I then had to say my due date, and then I had to explain why I'd only just realised. Naturally, any person of moderate curiosity will then ask why I've only just realised, and before I know it, I'm talking about my menstrual cycle to, like, my aunt or the guy from NatWest.

Factor in here that I had spent the whole of my pregnancy with T ranting on about how you could drink booze, how abstinence was for idiots who couldn't understand statistics, how only a jellyfish would give up soft cheese and pâté for a foetus, how the entire pregnancy industry had snowballed around this cold flint of intention, to freak women out needlessly. I'm not exactly going back on all of that, but it does help, with pregnancy, to at least know you're pregnant. Yes, have a drink, while you're pregnant, but don't be drunk. Both my sister and my friend A claimed to have drunk whatever they liked when they were pregnant with their second. I was touched in one way at the lengths they would go to make me feel better. And yet at the same time, I was there. I did know them both then. So I do know they were talking bollocks.

I had forgotten, as well, about the incessant worrying. As soon as I found out, I was worrying about why it wasn't moving. And then it started moving, and wouldn't stop, and I thought maybe it had ADHD (had I given it foetal ADHD with all the booze?). I said that to my sister, and she said, "It might be because it's a girl." So then I was worried that it was a girl (correctly, as it turned out – though I needn't have worried. Girls are fabulous. I thought when she was born, I must be careful not to tar her with my own feelings of feminine inadequacy, I must make sure I do not favour T just because he is different. Ha! What I didn't realise until I had a daughter was the profundity of my self-love. You'd think I'd have known that for years, that "extraordinary self-satisfaction" would be on my CV between my basic hygiene certificate and knowing how to drive. No, I thought I preferred the masculine to the feminine. I thought my sense of self was as a defective man. Was it arse!)

Anyway, then I was worried that I hadn't been tired enough in the first trimester, that the baby hadn't been a very effective parasite, since it hadn't totally drained me. In fact I had been totally drained, but I was so sludgy I'd forgotten everything – the whole atmosphere of the previous four months had just misted over. It is unbelievable to me that I didn't notice until so late – if I go back and read the columns that I wrote in that first trimester, it is as plain as the great ugly nose on my face. It's a ceaseless flow of arguments, confusion, untoward events that would never normally happen, missed deadlines and things left on buses. It reads like a person taking an A-level in incompetence, having to cover many modules: incompetence (finance); incompetence (traffic and public transport); incompetence (personal relationships)...

For about two weeks, there was a small amount of exhilaration to be had from the fact that I only had to live with half a pregnancy, rather than a whole one. This wore off amazingly quickly, and when I got to the sixth month I was exactly as bored and vexed and hot as I had been the time before. There is no way on earth to measure this, so all I can tell you is how it felt: it genuinely did not go any faster, even though you could look at it as if I'd had a head start of 20 weeks.

Plus, even though to me I was due exactly the same amount of whining, and worrying, and banging on, that is not how the world greets a second pregnancy. Love, nobody is interested in your second pregnancy (they should print that on a T-shirt, and then the kind of person who wears one saying "I just don't care about climate change!" could buy one for laundry days). To the not-pregnant, to the outsider – even, I suspect, the outsider who is only partially outside, like, for instance, its father – you are just doing that thing you've already done, again. Like you've had your bathroom done up, and they listened to you complaining about pipes all the way through that, and now they have to hear the whole lot again because you're doing the downstairs loo? Are you serious?

There is an awful lot, indeed almost everything, that you'll learn from experience when the baby is right there in front of you. I say that, though of course I'd forgotten all the things that would have been helpful, so having a second baby was more like being reminded of the time I had a dream about having a baby. But the pregnancy and labour are actually made worse with the repetition.

You worry more: the first time, if they'd told me my bump was too small and maybe the baby wasn't growing properly, I would have thought that just meant I was nice and slim. Never mind about the baby, I would have thought. Maybe he/she will be nice and slim as well. Of course, once you've done it, and realised how hair-raising it is even when they're 100% healthy, you cannot brook the smallest hint of malaise, not the faintest breath, not even a midwife measuring you with a tape measure, when you strongly dispute how accurate this is as a test of what's going on inside, and you suspect anyway that she's trying to wind you up as a punishment for being late. That aspect, especially in the late stages – which, given the circumstances, was pretty much all of it – was far, far worse. H wasn't small at all, by the way, even though my measurements were a full four centimetres out. I honestly believe that they haven't even *standardised* the point on your stomach that they measure from, but never mind.

I was absolutely convinced that on August 5, in accordance with my due date, I would be delivered of a baby boy that we would call either Stirling or Gulliver, depending on whether C was going to cave a little bit or cave completely.

I thought it was going to happen incredibly fast, because that's what happens to people who did OK the first time. (Do you see what's happened, by the way? My experience of labour has morphed from "the worst thing, by a million miles, that has ever happened to me, including the time when I got run over and I saw my own thigh bone through my leg" to "I did OK". That, right there, is the survival of the species.) The second one slips out like a wet piglet – it happens so fast you don't even have time to breathe properly or swear at people, you just have to hold tight and hope it doesn't come on your garden path or in the footwell of your car.

Even if you didn't do OK the first time, even if you had an emergency c-section, the chances are that the second time will be a) fine and b) incredibly fast.

August 3 lumbered up, and I had the mildest sensation of labour. It was a kind of sitcom labour, not painful enough for you to raise your voice or a sweat, but sufficiently perceptible that you would put on a hospital gown and gather your five closest friends around you in a hospital (I am thinking, specifically, of the sitcom Friends). T had shown no interest at all in my gravid condition. Other children his age would pat their mothers, or say "baby" or "sister" or something, anything, to indicate that they knew there was something in there besides bagels. I thought at the time maybe he was in denial, but I think now that *I* was in denial, so anxious about the whole thing that I wasn't just under-encouraging, I didn't just fail to read There's a House in My Tummy (though I did, also, fail to do this), I actively averted all talk of it. I created an atmosphere in which the possibility of a baby couldn't be mentioned. It makes you realise how subtle and yet incredibly unsubtle your influence can be, in your own house, on your own family. How can I have only just realised that?

Immediately, we whizzed T over to my sister's, and came home. I remember cleaning the cutlery drawers and complaining a lot that it wasn't happening fast enough, and also that it hurt. The next day was just a tedious, anxious blur of concocting physical activities, walking the dog up and down the hill, cleaning the other cutlery drawer, complaining more... Nothing much happened, and I went back to bed. T was still at my sister's. I should have just gone to get him. Or got him back. Or just gone to hang out – she only lives 20 minutes away from me. All these things I could have done, but I was still absolutely positive that the birth, when it finally came upon me, would be almost instantaneous, somewhere, lengthwise, between a fake tan and a pedicure.

At three in the morning, we went in to hospital. On the way there, we saw this friend; since you ask, it was one of the people we went to New York with, the time I was incredibly bad-tempered, and they still like C more than me. He'd been out on the lash and was having a cigarette outside his house when we walked past, and C stopped for a chat. Somewhere at the back of my mind, I was thinking, "This isn't right. If I were really in active labour, I would not be standing here, smiling mildly, while C has a conversation about how come the Tim Bobbin stays open till three in the morning. Yes, there were things I *was* thinking, like, "You can check the opening times of that and indeed all the pubs in our area, on the internet, when we have completed this small task of giving birth", but I wasn't furious. I wasn't like a woman possessed, and that is what you're supposed to be if it's all going right.

Huh, this is because it wasn't going right. Nothing was going anywhere. We had hours and hours of nothing going anywhere, and of course I'd written an incredibly strident thing about wanting all the drugs on my birthing plan, so we didn't even have a nice view. The morning shift started, and still nothing. I was missing T like crazy; that was all I could think about. I partly want to file this under "crazy notions you get while you're in labour", but actually, we hadn't been away from him for longer than one night his entire life. Even though he, as well as the dog, will on occasion prefer my sister to me (once he moved me out of the way so he could sit next to her), it still didn't feel right. It didn't feel like three days was nothing, just a trifling amount of time he wouldn't notice.

Still nothing happened.

I remember thinking, "God, gas and air is nothing like as much fun as I remember it." I recall formulating those exact words in my head. And yet, if you were to ask me now what gas and air was like, all I can remember is how much fun it is. Yik yak yik yak, things continued not to happen. I had my precious epidural (they are good, I must say), and a while after that, the room emptied suddenly, and I was on my own. Quite a young obstetrician came in and said to nobody, or maybe there was someone behind her, "Is she all right? She looks a bit hot." I said, "I'm not hot – I'm just a bit upset." (I wanted to go home, and see T, and not be pregnant). "Don't be upset," she said brightly. Which made me laugh, though not for very long.

Just as suddenly, the room was incredibly full: it was like a cocktail party full of people in very plain, collarless clothes. It was like a Chinese cocktail party. A doctor said, "This baby isn't going to come out vaginally", and then looked at me, expectantly, like I might have a better idea. I still had it so fixed in my head that ob-gyn doctors try and steer you away from a c-section, it didn't occur to me that maybe *he* was suggesting a caesarean and was braced for the fact that

207

I might object. When I finally twigged, I was so relieved that he actually had a plan, that he wasn't waiting for me to have one, that I tried to wave away the consent forms. Oh my dear, of course you must do whatever you think right – don't mind me and my silly consent.

The whole operation is fine. I mean, sure, it's disgusting, but it's fine. They say it's like someone rummaging around in a handbag, and I suppose that is what you'd say, if for some crazy reason you were trying to avoid saying, "It's like someone rummaging around in your stomach." When they get the baby out, they put it on your neck, so you can hug it. With your neck. That is totally unsatisfactory, but I guess this has been refined over decades of operations. They really can't win: you can't use your arms, and if they just whip the baby away till later, people get really cross.

They put up a sheet to stop you seeing anything during the operation itself, which the woman in the bed next to me (afterwards, in post-natal) said she had got round by watching the whole thing in the reflective silver panels on the surgery doors. Too late, she realised she was going to be sick, and she saw her own stomach going into spasm. It was sitting on the table beside her.

But I didn't do that. I was fine. The morning after, the obstetrician came round. I think he'd mistaken me for an old hippy who wanted a homebirth – perhaps because I am old – because he quite sternly said, "This delivery never would have happened naturally: if you'd been at home, you would have been in real trouble."

"I never wanted her at home," I replied. "Pretty much the only thing to be said for this whole performance is that my waters didn't break on my own carpet."

"Really?" he said, diverted momentarily from the tedium of his rounds by the possibility that I might be mad. "The *only* thing?"

"Well, no, no," I corrected. "The only thing apart from this *beautiful baby*…"

I came out thinking I'd failed. Worse, I'd failed at a test I'd actually passed before. I'd doubly failed. Then I thought, right, this is what people mean when they talk about post-natal euphoria – that's the bit you don't get when you have the operation instead of the warrior-style birthing experience. Then I thought, oh no, what if she notices that I'm not as euphoric as I was with T?

Then I remembered that I had exactly the same – I mean *exactly* the same – nebulous, indefinable sense of failure when I had T. Even though that was a textbook birth, and nothing could have gone any differently without being worse, I still emerged, even through all the crackling bliss, with a lapsarian sense not just of inadequacy but of loss, as if I had done something wrong and lost something important, for ever. I think it's just crackpot body-talk. I think maybe your placental output is more than just blood supply: it boosts your platelets with a sense of your own power and success. And then that goes, leaving behind, once more, this beautiful baby.

She came out looking exactly, uncannily like T. Then she went through a phase during which, if I'd told you she was the result of an affair with Ray Winstone, you wouldn't have been surprised. And now she is a peach, from every possible angle.

That's what you can never believe, before you embark on this: how much you're going to love them. You think, "Well, I don't like anybody else's. Why should I feel so strongly about mine?"

I just don't know. I do not have even a fraction of the answer. Well, of course I know why I feel so strongly about mine. Mine are perfect.

ACKNOWLEDGEMENTS

For letting me rip off their stories, quote and misquote them, poorly disguise them, impute thoughts and motives to them that I never checked, and outrageously misrepresent them, offering no right of reply, I would like to thank/seek the absolution of: Gwen Evans, Stacey Williams, Will Lee, Dixie Lee, Dot Lee, Ian Jepps, Pauline Jepps, Julia Jepps, David Jepps, Emilia Jepps, Julia Walsh, Jeremy Hayward, Ben Rowell, Marie O'Riordan, Adam Laycock, Dominic Nooney, Tamsin Nooney, Charlotte Moore, Tommy Bouchier Hayes, Richard Williams, Jan Williams, Sophie Williams, Philippa Lowe, Elodie Gutierrez, Tim Lusher, Peter Rhodes, Pete Martin, Jill Wooster, Damon Syson, Bethan Ryder, Clare Maugham, Polly Russell, Claire Birchall, Emma Wilkinson, Terry Ramsey, Liz McGlynn, Alex O'Connell, Jules Bueno, Laura Cumming, Hilla Sewell, Thea Sewell, Mo White, Paul Hilder, Rachel Essex, Rebecca Fox, Sacha Teulon, Kit Lynch-Robinson, Victoria Shepherd, Michelle Rae, Clare Drayton, Christian Adams, Eliane Glaser, Nicola Kohn, Andrew Billen, Lucy Billen, Abigail Billen, Jenny Evans,

Daniel Stroll, Lucinda Stroll and Benjamin Stroll. For getting me started, and then not sacking me, Kath Viner. And some other people who didn't sack me and/or were encouraging: Emily Wilson, Clare Margetson, Paula Cocozza, Amy Fleming, Lisa Darnell, Rob Fearn. For his relentless high spirits: Phil Daoust.

INDEX